BEYOND THE GOAL

The Biography of

BAICHUNG BHUTIA

BEYOND THE GOAL

The Biography of

BAICHUNG BHUTIA

MOHAMMAD AMIN-UL ISLAM

RANDOM HOUSE INDIA

Published by Random House India in 2014
1

Random House Publishers India Pvt. Ltd.
7th Floor, Infinity Tower C
DLF Cyber City
Gurgaon 122 002, Haryana
India

Random House Group Limited
20 Vauxhall Bridge Road
London SW1V 2SA
United Kingdom

978 81 8400 5233

Typeset in Garamond Premier Pro by Saanvi Graphics, Noida

Printed and bound in India by Replika Press Pvt. Ltd, India

A PENGUIN RANDOM HOUSE COMPANY

To the memory of my father, who never missed a football match at the Maidan

Contents

Foreword

When I was not yet a star, Baichung was already a big name in Indian sports. We both belong to the North-east and that's how we connect well. I think he is the first modern superstar from the North-east who made it big at the international level much before Dingko Singh's gold-medal feat at the 1998 Bangkok Asian Games, which inspired me to take up boxing.

Baichung's hard work and struggle say a lot about his success in modern sports.

I don't remember which year it was, but I watched Baichung for the first time when he was playing in a Santosh Trophy match. I don't remember the venue. Thereafter, I watched most of the national team matches on TV, particularly the two Nehru Cup finals in Delhi in 2007 and 2009.

I appreciate Baichung's selfless approach to life. He has done a lot to promote football in the country and in Sikkim. I strongly believe that for iconic sportspersons, contributing to society at large should be one of their responsibilities. He has done that of his own accord, without being told about his role when he retired from the sport.

Both of us come from nondescript villages and had some common goals to develop our respective sports in India. I haven't been to Tinkitam, but I think it can be compared with Manipur's Kangathei village, from where I hail.

I understand how hard it was to make his way up, given the lack of facilities that he must have faced as a youngster. His vision to develop the sport through his academy and club remind me of my own academy which I had launched in 2007 to cater to the needs of Manipur's underprivileged young girls and boys.

Baichung didn't want to see his state get left behind in football and made the dreams of so many young Sikkimese players come true.

Like all of us from the North-east, Baichung is an unassuming person who never threw his weight around. Success didn't change him. He is the same person that he was even a decade ago, modest and grounded. That's what makes him so likeable.

He is one of India's best sportspersons and remains a model for the youth of the country.

Mary Kom

Sunil Chhetri on Baichung

Ever since I have understood football, Baichung *bhai* has been my idol. Besides being a great player, I think he is a gem of a person. For me, he has always been like an elder brother who guided me through thick and thin in my career. In 2002, when I went to Calcutta as a 19-year-old to play for Mohun Bagan, I was thrilled that I would play alongside him.

Bhai was the biggest influence on my generation of players. A great motivator, he never imposed his stardom on the junior players.

His amazing confidence was another thing that I really admired. Even when the chips were down, he wouldn't throw in the towel. As a leader, he was our guiding force and encouraged us to fight back. As a player, he was dedicated and honest, and never shied away from taking responsibilities. I think it came naturally to him.

Bhai gave cent per cent in whatever he did, be it in scoring goals or winning *Jhalak Dikhhla Jaa*. He is a true winner who dedicated everything to the beautiful game. Even after his retirement, he didn't want to relax, but wanted to promote the game at the grass-roots level. United Sikkim Club was his novel idea as he sincerely felt that young players from his state should not be left out in the race.

Last year in November, I was delighted when I surpassed him as India's top scorer with forty-three goals. It was a great feeling. He came down from the stands and congratulated me. He's somebody whom I've always respected and emulated on the playing field.

I sincerely thank him for everything, from the moment I was chosen for the national team till now.

He is a legend and an icon who has inspired so many youngsters like me. It was an honour playing in a national team which had Baichung Bhutia in it.

I'm sure that when I grow old, I'll proudly tell everyone that I had once played alongside him.

Preface

On a hot and sunny June afternoon when my father was preparing to leave for the Maidan, I made up my mind that I wanted to be taken along.

He was in a fix, initially, but relented. We drove down in his Standard car from our central Calcutta home to the Maidan—the hotbed of India's football capital.

In 1977 I was only six, but I clutched my father's hand and stood on the rickety wooden stands of the Mohammedan Sporting gallery. The fans were in a state of delirious joy and held their umbrellas high in the air. I only heard, 'Habib, Habib'; Habib was one of India's top stars in that era.

My dad whispered, 'Habib has scored a *goal*.'

At that age when my life revolved around Tintin, Mandrake, Lothar and Phantom, the technicalities of football seemed like geometrical theorems.

All I retain about that 'goal' is a sense of joy and contentment.

In the late 1970s and 80s, some of the best moments of middle-class families in Calcutta were spent watching Mohun Bagan, East Bengal, and Mohammedan Sporting on black and white TV sets on weekends.

If there was a power cut, the running commentary in Ajay Bose's mellifluous voice on the ubiquitous Murphy radio provided succour. His diction and inimitable style made football commentary a highly enjoyable experience. Besides, the multiple Bengali football magazines, some copies of which I still possess, added to the entertainment.

When I became a freelance journalist in 1993, the same year that Baichung debuted in Calcutta, I visited various clubs which brought me closer to the game. But sadly, football witnessed a downslide in popularity. Even my late dad's interest had dwindled after the retirement of some of the biggest stars from the 1970s and 80s who had added glamour to the game. Another reason for his declining interest was the 1982 and 1986 FIFA World Cups which were beamed live in India. After watching high quality matches in the 1982 and 1984 Nehru Cups, which had former World Cuppers, he completely lost interest in the local league. The game crawled at a snail's pace.

My father never liked the idea of travelling to Salt Lake Stadium as he felt it lacked the Maidan's charisma. But when Baichung came to Calcutta and there was a buzz, his interest was revived. 'How's he as a player? Is he really good like Chuni or Habib?' he asked.

I nodded in affirmation and told him that Baichung a scored 'goals' with elegant back-volleys like Shyam Thapa.

My dad watched the 1997 Federation Cup semifinal agai Mohun Bagan on TV. Baichung's amazing speed and hat-tri reminded him of Habib's younger brother Mohammad Akb and Subhash Bhowmick, he said.

In the last few years of his life, he repented that he could watch Baichung at the Maidan.

Today, I feel a void within me when I think that he is n around to read Baichung's biography and have a chance meet him.

I love him for introducing me to this great game.

Mohammad Amin-ul Isla
June 201

1

Family and Childhood

Who is Ugen Sangey?

Few Indian football fans would recognize this name. Even a Google search might leave you disappointed. Ugen Sangey is one of the best-kept secrets of the football world.

I was astonished to learn that Ugen Sangey is Baichung Bhutia's real name. I didn't know it for many years despite my interactions with him. Of course, knowing his introverted nature, it isn't surprising that Baichung didn't open up about this. There are sides to him so private that not even those in the village in which he grew up know about them.

I learned this during a chance conversation with Kunzang Doma Bhutia, Baichung's elder sister.

'Is Ugen his actual name?' I asked her, amazed.

'Yes, it is,' she replied. 'Baichung is his pet name and we often used to call him Ugen, his official name.'

When little Baichung joined school and was asked his name, he rolled out his pet name which means 'the little one'—and it stuck.

To understand Baichung's roots better, I decided to travel to his home state, Sikkim, in December 2001 when he was there recovering from a knee injury after a stint in England. It was my maiden visit to Sikkim and his village, Tinkitam, was completely unknown to me. Earlier that month, when Baichung was in Delhi, he had invited me to visit Tinkitam. A travel plan had been finalized—I would visit his village after Christmas, where he would be spending a week with his parents. However, I had no mobile or any phone number on which I could contact him. He had only given me a rough sketch of the route, but, as I realized later, it wasn't that easy to reach a remote village in south Sikkim.

I boarded the Rajdhani Express to Calcutta and, the following evening, I took the Darjeeling Mail from Sealdah station to New Jalpaiguri with a waitlisted ticket. I tried telling the TT that I was a journalist from Delhi; unfortunately, it didn't carry much import. But once the train chugged out of the platform, he let me stay on board.

As night approached, I took out a blanket and rolled it out near the toilet. As I lay there, I tried to distract myself from the stench by thinking about Baichung and Tinkitam and what awaited me there. The next morning, I walked down to the Tenzing Norgay bus stand near the New Jalpaiguri station. I still didn't know where Tinkitam was and how I would get there. I found out from a bystander that I first needed to go to

Gangtok and then get a connecting cab to my destination, but he didn't mention the route!

After reaching Gangtok, I faced another problem. Nobody knew the exact location of Tinkitam. I walked up and down the Mall Road for a couple of hours, making frantic efforts to meet some officials at the Sikkim Football Association (SFA) office. But it was a Saturday and the office was shut.

It was getting dark and I almost lost hope. As a last-ditch effort, I made some calls to my journalist friends in Calcutta from a phone booth to find out if Baichung was even in Sikkim. I couldn't get any concrete leads. It was then that a middle-aged lady who had overheard my conversation at the booth approached me.

'Are you looking for Baichung's address? I'm going towards Ravangla where his sister lives. You can go to her house if that would help you,' she said. It was as though, given the hill's mystic surroundings, this lady popped up from nowhere with a ray of hope for me.

At last, a ray of hope

I gratefully hopped on to a jeep with her and we set off for Ravangla in south Sikkim. During our journey she mentioned three names—Ganju Lama, Danny Denzongpa and Baichung Bhutia—that have made Sikkim proud.

'They're the three famous sons of Sikkim,' she said.

I had watched Danny Denzongpa's first-ever Bengali movie, *Lal Kuthir*, in the late 1970s. Danny, who is related to Baichung on his mother's side, was already famous in Bollywood then.

Ganju Lama, who was born in Sangmo in south Sikkim on 22 July, 1924, was the first of the famous Sikkimese to fight in the Second World War and earn a Victoria Cross with the British Gurkha Rifles. And since 2001, Baichung has been earning laurels as a football pro. I thought I knew a lot about Baichung already, but I learned much about the two other famous sons of Sikkim from her.

The sun had set behind the majestic Kanchenjunga as the jeep took the winding road up the hill. The lady instructed the driver to drop me at Ravangla as she had to get off early. I thanked her for her timely support—Tinkitam, I was told, was only an hour's drive from Ravangla. Upon reaching the quieter Ravangla at 7 p.m., I realized it was too late an hour to approach Baichung's sister. Hence I retired to a small hotel, where I asked a local driver, Dilip, if he knew where Tinkitam was. This time the response was heartening. He nodded vigorously and exclaimed, 'Who doesn't know Tinkitam?' When I told him that I was a journalist and wanted to see Baichung, he was ready to be my guide.

'I haven't met Baichung. Can I have a snap with him?' Dilip asked eagerly. It seemed to me that for any commoner in Sikkim, meeting the star footballer at his birthplace was a once-in-a-lifetime experience.

I dropped the idea of meeting Baichung's sister in the morning because that would mean losing time. Also, I wasn't really aware of Baichung's other commitments. Dilip and I set off the following morning at 5 a.m. to catch Baichung before he moved out of his village to meet his friends and relatives.

The hour-long drive from Ravangla was quite pleasant except for the bumpy, uneven roads.

After driving for an hour, Dilip said, 'We have to walk 2 kilometres from here because the car can't go beyond this point.'

A sleepy hamlet

Set against the backdrop of the Kanchenjunga, Tinkitam is ethereal in its beauty. With no telephones, cable networks or vehicles, the sleepy hamlet looked like a village out of a postcard. The 2-kilometre stretch that led to Baichung's house was flanked by lush green cardamom plantations. We ventured ahead, braving the cold early morning winds that numbed our senses and the rocky path that made our knees tremble.

On the way, I found a boy filling a bucket with water. As I did not know Nepali or Sikkimese, I simply asked him, 'Baichung? Baichung?' The little boy pointed to a house some distance away. We had walked that way for just a few minutes when two boys came scampering up the path, kicking a football. They didn't notice us, absorbed as they were in the game. Upon nearing the house, the eerie silence was broken by Dinko, the Bhutia family's Tibetan mastiff, who greeted me with a quick, scary search. Baichung's elder brother Rapden stepped in just in time and I heaved a sigh of relief. Close behind was Baichung, walking with the help of a crutch, but cheerful and enthusiastic all the same.

At first sight, he seemed to me like a wounded tiger. I looked admiringly at his feet that had thwarted so many defenders and scored so many goals. When I told him how lucky he was to be born and raised in the cradle of nature, Baichung, who now stays in Gangtok, confessed that he found it difficult to stay there for more than a week.

'Tinkitam is so quiet,' he smiled.

Baichung or Bhaichung, a spelling he uses often, was born to Sonam Topden Bhutia and Dorji Doma Bhutia in a Buddhist Bhutia family in Tinkitam on 15 December, 1976. At the age of six, he already knew what he wanted in life—to play football and only football. He started playing with his friends and siblings in the open spaces in the village where he was born and raised. Being the youngest in the family, he was loved and adored by his elder brothers, Rapden Bhutia and Chewang Ongdup Bhutia, and his only sister, Kunzang. Nobody else in his family has ever played professional football, but the sport—along with basketball—has always been popular in the North-east.

'He used to get along very well with other boys of his age, and would happily play with them. They were mostly kids of the part-time farmers who used to till our land,' Rapden said.

On Sundays and during vacations, the Bhutias would have family get-togethers in which football figured prominently. 'His love for football began at home. My brothers and our domestic helps would all play a game in the evening. We've always loved football,' said Chewang, who works as a manager in a restaurant in Sydney, Australia.

On our way back from Tinkitam, Baichung wanted to come along with me as he had to meet friends at Namchi, which is a

30-minute drive from his village. On the way he showed me a stadium named after him. It was followed by a brief visit to his sister's place in Ravangla where I unearthed a treasure trove of memories over a plate of steaming home-cooked momos, the staple diet of the Sikkimese people.

'He was very sporty and instinctive. As a kid, he liked to watch both football and cricket,' said his sister, Kunzang, who now stays at Luing near Gangtok after her family shifted from Ravangla in 2002.

'He was not chubby at all, and quite fit. We used to play football almost every evening. And he was a crybaby. Whenever his team lost, he made sure that the game went on for extra time until he won!' laughed Kunzang. 'We used to have disagreements and he used to cry. I believe he had a competitive spirit and a passion for winning from a very young age,' she said.

His former coaches say that the desire to win, ingrained in him early on, kept him going. He would not let any obstacle block his path. Though puny and skinny, he had pace and skill. Most of his school friends and teachers remember not only his will to win but also the effect it had on his teammates.

Baichung would not take a poor team performance quietly; he would be disturbed by the failure and his instinctive reaction would be to encourage his teammates, whether at the Boys Club or at his school, Tashi Namgyal Academy (TNA), to turn things around.

At Tinkitam, when I inquired about his parents, Rapden walked towards the cardamom fields and waved at a couple engrossed in instructing the workers there. His parents had their hands full with the cardamom fields that flanked their house on the foothills of the Kanchenjunga. While Chewang is settled abroad and Baichung in Gangtok, Rapden, who used to be a teacher in a primary school, has always stayed with his parents in their ancestral village.

Like most other elderly women in the state, Baichung's mother was dressed in the traditional Sikkimese Bokhu. And like the others in her family, the bespectacled lady didn't go overboard while narrating her struggle and the sacrifices she and her husband made while raising four children in a place like Tinkitam, where modern facilities were rare in the 1970s.

Instead, the couple flashed that thousand-watt smile which seemed to speak volumes about how contented they were.

'He wasn't a temperamental or lazy child. He's always been a good boy, as quiet and shy as he is today. I'm happy for him and feel proud of him. He shaped his own future and brought so much respect to our family. Now I feel that the worry and fear was worth it because he got to do what he loves the most and what makes him happy,' Baichung's mother recounted. 'But my eyes have hardly seen him grow. He has done our family proud, but I also used to feel a void. I didn't get to know how my son became a man. It makes me sad at times.'

'In the beginning, we were a little worried that football would get in the way of his education,' his father told me. But he was happy to see his youngest son's amazing success in football.

Unfortunately, his father passed away on 6 December, 2012. Baichung was then in Delhi. His father's death created a void in his life. Though he never talked about it to his friends or in public, the loss was irreparable as only he knew how much his dad had sacrificed to raise him and his siblings and give them all that they wanted in life.

Baichung and his brother took me to his room which still had a few framed memories. Rapden pointed out one particular photo that enjoyed pride of place: 'That was when he got selected by SAI.'

Most kids would not like the idea of leaving their home and parents, but little Ugen was already prepared for a life away from home. He quietly left the comfort of his home at the age of five to embark on an uncharted journey. But sending her youngest kid off to a hostel had tormented his mother.

'As a mother, dropping a kid off at boarding school at such a young age was an awful feeling. I used to wonder how and when he would eat and sleep. I used to be tense most of the time. But when he left for Calcutta in 1993, I wasn't too worried because he was already seventeen then. Besides, in Calcutta there was a future for him in football and he was grown up enough to take care of himself,' she added.

'When you came to Calcutta as a young boy, did you ever feel lonely?' I asked Baichung.

'I have been away from home since the age of five. So I wasn't too sad about coming down to Calcutta. In the initial days, I stayed at Nager Bazar in an East Bengal official's rented flat. Adjusting to a new city and a new way of life was difficult, but I slowly got used to it,' reminisced Baichung.

'For a couple of months after he went to Calcutta to join the East Bengal team, he definitely felt lonely. But he quickly recovered. He's always been able to cope with his emotions,' said Rapden.

I've always wanted to fathom Baichung's mental strength on and off the field and have tried to gauge this every time I've met him. During important matches, he would always look intense and focussed, but never would he come across as a bundle of nerves.

Even after his fame and stardom began to grow, he kept himself from getting distracted by materialistic gains.

'He never lost his sense of reality. When he used to come from Calcutta, he would wander around the village as usual without any airs. That's why being famous, signing autographs, or taking photos with fans doesn't affect him,' his mother said. 'None of my children has lost touch with reality. We haven't moved to a different region. We've never wanted to leave our roots. The kids are the same as always. I hope they never change.'

My hour-long stay with the family of Indian football's most favourite son revealed a lot about the realities that comprise the lives of our sportspersons. How does it feel for an England-returned footballer to watch his ageing father till the land in a remote village in Sikkim? Champions in Indian sports grow up amid great hardship—this is an oft-told story of players from the far-flung areas of the country. And I believe that his modest background only burnished Baichung's determination to excel when he came to Calcutta.

Baichung's parents were initially unimpressed by his keen interest in sports. Their fears were put to rest by Karma Bhutia. Karma isn't related to Baichung's family but was his mentor, and later played a significant role in shaping his career.

'At that time, parents were not keen on encouraging their kids in sports. But Karma uncle convinced my parents that Baichung would manage both sports and studies,' said Kunzang.

At five, Baichung was sent to St Xavier's School in Pakyong, East Sikkim, where he was enrolled in Class I. It was here that he first showed signs of great skill.

'He was small-built but he impressed with his deft body movements and dribbling,' said a senior from his school, V. Chhetri.

Rise to prominence at Tashi Namgyal Academy

In 1986, when Baichung was ten, he won a football scholarship from Sports Authority of India (SAI) to attend Sikkim's best-known public school, TNA, in Gangtok. His love for the game grew at TNA.

When he reached seventh grade in 1989, the slightly built lad became a regular in the school football team. A year later, as he grew in size and skill, he began to outshine his teammates.

TNA gave him the space to excel as a player and supported him wholeheartedly in his endeavour, even allowing him to join football camps outside the state. Today, TNA basks in the glory of its most famous student who was once in their Yuksom (red) House.

'I remember how Yuksom House's only priority was to defeat Phensong (green) House, of which my friend Sherap Lepcha was a part,' said Baichung, who drew inspiration from Diego Maradona, Gary Linekar, and I.M. Vijayan.

Baichung earned his spurs the hard way. His school field, carved out of the rocky hills, had an undulating surface of sand and was smaller in size than a regular football ground. Only when he had an important match coming up did he train at Paljor Stadium.

His first football coach, Manas Chakraborty, who died in 2006, was also his biggest motivator and guide. Chakraborty, a SAI-certified football coach, was Baichung's first guru when he was a TNA student.

Chakraborty, a resident of Ghaziabad in Uttar Pradesh, had been training TNA students ever since he joined the school in 1987.

He once said that Baichung was the jewel in the crown of his football team.

'Baichung was the star in that famous school team of 1987. There were other talented boys like Sherap Lepcha, Simon Subba, Amber Thapa and Henry,' he had said. After TNA made it to the Subroto Cup quarterfinals in Delhi in 1992, all four got scholarships along with Baichung.

Baichung always respected the opinion of his school coaches. Even when he became a star player he never hesitated to seek their guidance. When, while playing for Mohun Bagan in 2002–03, Baichung's form dipped, the late coach was more worried than anyone else. Chakraborty had then said that East Bengal suited Baichung better as he was always in sparkling form when he played for them. Baichung recalled that when the school team played in outstation tournaments, Manas 'sir' was not only a friend, but also doubled as a partner-in-crime in pranks.

'Once when we travelled from Delhi to Ajmer for an inter-public school tournament, most of our players didn't have reserved tickets. Led by Manas sir, all of us threatened to travel on the roof. Finally, the TT gave us berths and the players came down. It was hilarious,' he recounted.

'For me it was like a father-son relationship,' said Baichung.

If Chakraborty saw the SAI scholar develop as a player, his biology teacher Leonard Lefevre and his house masters Lhagod Lama and Tashi Tenzing saw him grow from childhood into adolescence.

'He was extremely obedient. Despite his extremely busy football schedule, he never tried to bend the school rules,' said Lefevre.

The teachers confessed that Baichung's rise to stardom was far beyond their expectations.

'When he played for Sikkim XI against Mohun Bagan, we all felt he would do well in football but didn't expect that he would become this big a star,' said B. Parajuli, his former maths teacher.

Sherap and Simon, who later donned East Bengal and Peerless colours, were part of his gang. They have a treasure trove of memories about their friend, but what has struck them most about him is his love and affection for those he is close to.

'He hasn't changed a bit. He is the same old guy we used to know. Whenever he used to come to Sikkim from Calcutta he used to visit us in our hostel. He remained grounded. I remember him distributing T-shirts to the village kids,' said Sherap.

Lenny Sir and Yuksom House

If Karma shaped Baichung's football career, Leonard or Lenny sir, who taught him biology at TNA, has been one of the most important people in his life. The biology teacher fuelled his passion for football and never failed to encourage him whenever he did something impressive on the field. Baichung always fell back on Lenny and in letters written to him during his initial days in Calcutta, he shared with his teacher tales of his life and career in a new city.

Leonard was not a certified football coach, but had been a cricketer during his college days. He had an eye for spotting young talent and would guide them as best he could. Not many know about this, however, as he always kept a low profile. Leonard was in his final year of zoology at North Point, Darjeeling, when he went over to Gangtok to play in a cricket tournament. He was a talented all-rounder who also captained the college side and was the vice-captain of the district team.

'While in Gangtok, I heard that TNA was recruiting teachers. I appeared for the interview and, as fate would have it, I was asked to join work in February 1987,' he recalled.

Shortly afterwards, SAI adopted TNA as a school for their scholar students in five disciplines—football, swimming, athletics, badminton, and table tennis. Most of these students were raw and not up to the academic levels of the classes they were admitted into. The teachers were up in arms and predicted that all of them would fail.

'I volunteered to take these students under my wing. A separate SAI dorm was created for them and I was put in charge of the kids. It was a demanding and challenging task. I would be with them from 5.15 a.m., when the wake-up bell went off, till 9 p.m., when the lights would be turned off. This was apart from my normal twenty-six periods of teaching biology to students from Classes VI to X,' he said.

During the puja breaks and on long weekends, the hostel would empty out, but the SAI kids would stay back in Lenny sir's dormitory.

'Being pretty young myself, I was more like a big brother they could look up to and talk to without intimidation or fear of being judged harshly. I was close to all of them and especially to Baichung,' he added. 'He was pretty much my shadow and followed me everywhere, much like the pug in the Vodafone ad. Once our former principal Pramod Sharma remarked, "Lenny is just like one of the kids", as he'd often find Baichung and his gang hanging on to me like appendages,' he laughed.

Baichung's high confidence level convinced Leonard that he was destined to become a top sportsperson someday. He narrated an incident from the time when India co-hosted the cricket World Cup in 1987. Baichung was only eleven then. According to Leonard, it changed his perception of the youngster.

'It was the 10th of October and we were in the audio-visual room watching New Zealand play minnows Zimbabwe. The match was all but lost for Zimbabwe when Dave Houghton played a blinder of an innings. The game came down to the wire. The kids watched with rapt attention. Zimbabwe needed another 20 runs from 20-odd balls. Houghton sent the ball flying to the vacant long-on boundary. Everyone thought it was going to be a boundary, but Martin Crowe ran back with the ball coming over his shoulder and, near the boundary ropes, he flung himself to hold on to the most spectacular catch in the history of the game. I yelled out with excitement, "Great catch! Great catch!"

'Suddenly, there was a small voice that asked, "Sir, what's so great about that catch?" I looked down and saw a dishevelled Baichung. He was just about four feet tall and had recently joined TNA as a SAI scholar. We watched the TV replays and I explained to him how difficult it was to take a catch when running backwards, looking over one's shoulder,' the teacher explained.

The little boy, however, insisted that it was not a difficult catch and even boasted that he could do it. The teacher rebuked him and reminded him that he was a footballer who knew little about cricket. Leonard also told him that he wouldn't be able to take a catch as difficult as the one Crowe had taken. But Baichung would not give up—he accepted the challenge with modesty, much to the delight of his friends.

'Early next morning, I went to the cricket field and found Baichung and his band of friends eagerly waiting for me. I called him over to one side of the ground and explained to him that we would have to simulate the same conditions. I asked him to stand about 15 yards from where I was standing and face me as I would hit the ball in the air about 35 to 40 yards over his head. I told him he had to run back to chase and catch it. I hit the ball up in the air and he chased it. He didn't take his eyes off the ball for even a second and caught it clean,' Lenny reminisced.

'It was a fluke, I told him. So he came back with the ball and a big grin on his face. I challenged him to do it again. This time, I hit the ball even further and he actually had to fling himself full length at the end to take the catch. Afterwards, he did his usual cartwheels and somersaults to please his fans, who were delighted that "sir" has lost the challenge,' Lenny said with a smile.

Baichung's self-belief and confidence surprised the cricketer-cum-biology teacher.

'I had to eat humble pie. It wasn't just his athletic prowess. I knew for sure that he was different,' said Leonard, who left the school in 2006 to join his alma mater St Joseph's School in Darjeeling.

'As a child, he was always excited to learn new football tricks and worked hard to perfect them. I've even held on to the letters he wrote to me while he was away at the camps. They're part of my treasured collection now. Something told me even then that this child was destined for greatness,' he added.

For his juniors, Agya was a hero

Most students, including Baichung's seniors and juniors at TNA, considered him a superstar. They would often hang around, hoping to have a quick chat with him. He would always oblige with a modest smile.

One of the schoolmates inspired and encouraged by Baichung was Saurabh Chamling. Saurabh was in Class III when Baichung left school to join East Bengal in 1993. Baichung inspired him so much that he too decided to become a footballer. Though he played for his school, success did not court him in this field. However, he remained true to his passion and became a sports journalist, eventually joining the Goan club Churchill Brothers as its media officer.

'Agya (brother) was my senior in school. Having achieved success at a very young age, he was already a hero. I remember how my friends and I would run after him in school. We all wanted to talk to him. One day during lunch break, we saw Agya walking on campus. Wanting to make conversation, we asked him, "*Agya, kata janu bhako*? (Agya, where are you going)"', Saurabh recalled. 'He looked at us playfully and replied with a line from a Hindi song, "*Main toh chala jidhar chalay rasta*".'

Saurabh still remembers Baichung's last day at TNA.

'He was sad and downcast,' he continued. 'The school wanted to make a symbolic gesture and conducted his farewell assembly on the football ground where he had trained and played, instead of inside the auditorium.

'After the school song was sung, Agya was invited by the principal to share his thoughts with the students. I don't remember exactly what he said, but it was a short speech and in the end he said, "I'll miss the school".'

Sherap, who became best of friends with Baichung because of football, was two years junior to him in school. They first met during the SAI trials at TNA in 1986.

'He scored a beautiful back-volley goal. I've been his fan from that day on. Later, we became great friends and played in clubs in Calcutta,' he added.

As Leonard observed, while Baichung was like any other youngster his age, on the football pitch he was miles ahead. He had better control, and kicking and dribbling skills. The quickness of his feet combined with co-ordination and balance made him a joy to watch, even as a boy.

Frequently, opposition defenders were left cursing after being humiliated by his footwork. His pace was also an asset that he developed early and it gave him an advantage over others.

'He played for Yuksom House which was the weakest among all the teams. He was the only decent player in the team and almost every time he used to take the entire responsibility upon himself,' said Leonard.

Besides football, Baichung also dabbled in other sports, particularly cricket.

'During a tournament at Rangpur, I lost three of my players, including the wicketkeeper. Baichung volunteered to keep wickets for the team. Such has been his spirit,' Leonard said.

If he was fabulously brilliant in football, Baichung was also good in studies.

'He was a good student. He liked mathematics and did better in English compared to the performance of other students. He was a quick learner, which came in useful. Though he always stayed away from school for football camps, he used to catch up quickly after rejoining his classes,' said Leonard.

After he made a name for himself by winning trophies for his school, Baichung soon became famous outside the TNA corridors. Both Leonard and Sherap quipped that this made him quite popular with the girls.

'The senior girls often used to invite him to the canteen and brought juices for him,' said Leonard. 'But he was shy and would just rush out of there after finishing the juice.'

His teenage life was also fun-filled, particularly the Sundays when he was not playing. Mornings would be spent in front of the TV watching the popular serial *Mahabharata* while the afternoons were laced with boyish fun.

'On Sunday afternoons, we used to put on our best clothes and roam near the girls' hostel. Baichung's football fame got him noticed and, in turn, us as well. Getting female attention at that age was a nice feeling,' Sherap said with a smile. 'There was one girl in the hostel that he used to like. He would ask me to go and chat her up, enumerating his virtues!'

Ugen, Samara, Keisha: Loves of his life

Many popular boys in school had multiple girlfriends, but not Baichung. In fact, when he established himself as a star in Calcutta, he met Madhuri Tipnis, niece of former chief of air staff A.Y. Tipnis. At a time when Facebook and Twitter did not exist and the rules of courtship were very different, Baichung got her name tattooed on his hand. They dated for seven years before finally tying the knot on 27 December, 2004.

'We first met in 1997 in Calcutta through a common friend. I didn't follow football and hardly knew him. I had seen his picture once in a newspaper which showed him being given fitness tips by Syed Nayeemuddin,' said Madhuri.

Marrying outside the Buddhist community is considered taboo and Baichung's mother was initially concerned. She believed that he was one of the most eligible bachelors in the country and could have married almost any girl from his own community.

'Oh yes, that's so true. When we met we were very young. I personally didn't want to make our affair public. But Baichung insisted that it was better to let his parents know about me so that they were mentally prepared for a future marriage,' she explained.

When Baichung lived in England from 1999–2001 during his stint with Bury FC, he would cook for himself but, Madhuri revealed, 'He is not very experimental with food. He eats whatever he gets. But he's very fond of momos.'

I asked her if he has a sweet tooth.

'Not really. He is not fond of sweets but likes jalebis and cakes.'

In 2010, Baichung became the father of twins, 'Ugen' Kalzang and Keisha Dolkar Bhutia, and a year later, his second daughter, Samara Dechen, was born. Interestingly, while Baichung was not known to the world by his official name, he was happy to name his son Ugen.

'It's a great feeling to become a father. It's an amazing experience,' he said.

But he made it clear to the world that he didn't want his son to become a footballer; he wanted him to become a tennis player instead.

'As a parent, I would want my kids to take up a sport which ensures a good future and good quality of life,' explained Baichung, who feels tennis has better facilities as a sport.

In his role as husband and father, Baichung's responsibilities have doubled but he carries out his duties effortlessly. In 2011, when an earthquake hit Sikkim and parts of Nepal and Tibet, Baichung walked for eight hours from his village and then took a bus, about 60 kilometres from the epicentre to reach his pregnant wife and 17-month-old twins in Gangtok.

Despite belonging to a family that belongs to the Tibetan Buddhist sect Nyingmapa, which is the oldest of the four major schools of Tibetan Buddhism, including Kagyupa, Sakyapa and Gelugpa, Baichung is an atheist because he believes that religion creates divisions and engenders hatred.

'I only believe in hard work and I've never prayed before any match but I have prepared myself mentally for the challenge. I believe in some higher power but have never really felt its presence,' he added.

His success story has not only boosted the state's tourism industry and made Tinkitam popular among tourists, it has also encouraged Sikkimese parents to push their kids into sports. Sikkimese youth now take pride in pursuing football as a career. So, it is not surprising to see that he is treated as a legend and an icon in his home town. After observing his immense popularity closely, I can safely say he is Indian football's 'Little Buddha'.

But Baichung stays grounded and hasn't forgotten what his parents, teachers and elders have taught him—to be generous and down to earth always.

'I'm a normal person and I want to be myself and stay relaxed. I get embarrassed when people ask me to take pictures with them,' confessed Baichung.

Baichung personifies the essence of the Sikkimese character. He is honest, modest and simple. In the end, his has been a story of sweat, sweat, and more sweat.

2

Karma's Wunderkid

Other than in his native country, Brazil, Waldemar de Brito has remained relatively unknown in the football world. But Brito, a former international who also played in the inaugural FIFA World Cup in 1934, made a significant contribution to football when he spotted and gifted a rare genius named Edson Arantes do Nascimento, nicknamed Pele, to the sport in 1954.

Interestingly, the story of Karma Bhutia, who is credited with the discovery of Baichung Bhutia from a remote village in Sikkim, is similar to that of Brito's. Very few have acknowledged the role played by Karma and how his *karma* did a world of good to football in India.

Karma was an integral part of Baichung's life. It was he who noticed the talent in the young boy and took him under his wing.

In the book *The Nowhere Men,* which is about football scouts, Michael Calvin writes about a tribe that does a selfless job and they, as Calvin puts it, 'supply the star system but remain resistant to it'. In Indian football, the late Achyut Banerjee, Sir Dukhiram (Umesh Chandra Mazumdar), Bagha Shome, and Amal Dutta have groomed many footballers, some of whom later became top stars. But today, they're almost forgotten.

Like them, Karma is central to the mythology of football. He, too, belonged to a group of faceless men who spotted raw talent. Other than in Sikkim and, to a small extent, in Calcutta, no one really knows who he is and how he worked with a group of young footballers in his native state. This chapter is a tribute to the tireless and selfless efforts of Karma who gave us a jewel like Baichung, a player who went on to entertain us for more than a decade with his sparkling skill and demeanour.

Karma did his schooling in Darjeeling's Mt Hermon School where he played football, cricket and hockey. In 1973, he went to Hyderabad to study mechanical engineering. When, after completing the course, he came back to Sikkim in 1978, he joined the government as an engineer and was soon promoted to principal chief engineer.

His love for football, however, remained untainted. Balancing his passion for the sport with his job, Karma would spend most of his days with young players from his state who he thought had the right talent, but needed to be nurtured and given the right exposure. He was responsible for promoting and extending the careers of many; unfortunately, hardly any club recognized the contribution of Karma and of others like him.

As Calvin rightly observed, 'There is no textbook for the scouts to follow; they receive no diploma for their appreciation of the alchemy involved in the creation of a successful player. They only possess the power of dreams.'

In fact, it was Karma's dream which motivated him to carry out an intense experiment with the young Sikkimese footballers.

Karma says that though he didn't play for his state or the country, he had an eye for spotting talent. As a young player he represented his university in both football and hockey, but he always possessed a shrewd footballing brain, as he would later prove when he coached and managed a group of youngsters in the Gangtok-based Boys Club. Outside of his school, this was the first club that Baichung joined as a precocious youngster.

Enter Karma

So the story goes back twenty-five years, to when Karma met a young Baichung in 1989—one of the watershed years in Indian football.

'Sikkim is one place where almost everyone knows everyone. We knew Karma uncle through Boys Club. He was the team manager and he really appreciated Baichung's game. That's how our family got to know him,' said Rapden, Baichung's elder brother.

Taking note of the boy's talent, Karma unearthed him from the hills where opportunities and facilities are limited to playing in inter-school tournaments and the annual Sikkim Governor's Gold Cup.

'He saw me when I was still in TNA, playing in different inter-school tournaments. He decided to induct me into his Boys Club where he coached me. Later, he put me in the junior squad,' Baichung remembers.

It was a fiercely competitive atmosphere as Baichung sought to outperform his friends. Yet the nature of all the matches was informal and free of pressure, which allowed the youngsters to develop their individual strengths and unique style of play.

'Baichung joined the Boys Club in 1989 as a 13-year-old. I had been in charge of the club since 1988 as I, along with some of my friends, wanted to promote the game in my state. Most of these boys, including Baichung, used to stay at my place during the holidays. My wife used to rustle up quick nourishing refreshments for them, like banana shake, eggs, and soaked gram. The idea was to keep them in one group so as to create a sense of togetherness in the team,' Karma explained. 'When Baichung joined our team in 1989, I noticed that he outshone the other boys in terms of skills and determination.'

Herein lies Karma's greatest skill—though he never claimed to be a top-notch coach, he certainly had an eye for talent. Another player he spotted apart from Baichung was his best friend, Sherap.

Little Baichung, Karma noted, was highly motivated and possessed a killer instinct in his game. He only needed polishing, first under Karma and later under other coaches, for his career to catapult to success.

When he saw the potential in this driven teen, Karma decided to take him under his wing. As a mentor, he was aware that the boy was destined for success as a footballer. 'I knew he was special and my sixth sense told me that he would go places because he had the right temperament along with the right skills,' Karma said proudly. Slowly he was absorbed into the team which participated in various age-group tournaments. That's how Baichung kicked off his enviable career from his state.

Baichung started his education in St Xavier's School, Pakyong, East Sikkim, and eventually won a scholarship from SAI to attend TNA which is quite renowned in this part of the world.

'He was a batch junior to me. When I was in Class XII at Tashi Namgyal Senior Secondary School (TNSSS), he was in Class XI at TNA. He was always kicking a football around. I still remember watching him play against our school team. It was 1992–93. The matches between us were nothing short of an India–Pakistan cricket match as neither of the teams wanted to lose,' said Shital Pradhan, a former student at TNSSS, whose football team played against the formidable TNA.

Unlike that of the others in his group, Baichung's rise was steady. Beginning with the all-India school games, he graduated to sub-junior, junior, and senior national tournaments. His spectacular talent earned laurels for TNA as he excelled in all the public school tournaments and the Subroto Cup in 1992, which brought him attention from the national media.

'TNSSS never had players of the calibre of Sherap, the twins Ram and Laxman, and Baichung. They were a strong team and won many trophies. Baichung was already a star in his school and in the Boys Club, the most popular team in Gangtok. In 1993, he shifted to Calcutta and never looked back. Today when I read about him, I feel proud to have seen this legend from a young age,' Pradhan added.

Baichung led TNA to win the Indian Public Schools' Conference (IPSC) football tournament in 1990 and 1991. He was declared the best player of the tournament at Mayo College, Ajmer, in 1991.

'Tero Daichung lay pura naam kamaocha'

While the late Manas Chakraborty trained him at TNA, Thupden Rapgyal was Baichung's coach at the club. In 1992, his performance in the Subroto Cup in New Delhi earned him a spot in the under-16 national team for a tournament in Dhaka, Bangladesh. The same year, he represented Sikkim XI in the Sikkim Governor's Gold Cup at Gangtok's Paljor Stadium.

'I had gone to Paljor Stadium with my grandfather to watch the semifinal between Sikkim Football Association (Blue) and Mohun Bagan,' said Saurabh Chamling, a junior of Baichung's at TNA.

'The atmosphere was electrifying and the stadium was full as a local team had qualified for the quarterfinals. Agya didn't play as a striker, but as an attacking midfielder. He ran a lot, won the balls and then made inroads into the Mohun Bagan defence and challenged their Nigerian defender Christopher Kem,' Saurabh added.

After a goalless first half, SFA earned a free kick after a Bagan player fouled on Baichung.

'Devendra Gurung, another product of TNA, took a swinging shot which beat the Bagan goalkeeper. But the joy was short-lived as Bagan equalized to take the match into tie-breaker, which they won,' he added.

'I still remember my grandfather told me that day, "*Tero Daichung lay pura naam kamaocha, ekdum ramro khelda raicha* (Your Daichung will make a name for himself, he's playing very well.)" He used to mispronounce Baichung as Daichung.'

In fact, it was not just Saurabh's grandfather who took note of young Baichung that day at Paljor Stadium. He was a bright prospect. The visiting clubs from Calcutta and the local fans acknowledged his talent as his team reached the semifinals where they went down to the eventual winners, Mohun Bagan, during extra time.

Despite the defeat, Baichung didn't break down as he knew that winning and losing were part of the game.

Initially, Karma wasn't too keen on throwing a young Baichung into the cauldron of expectations and refused to release him to represent Sikkim XI in the Governor's Gold Cup in 1990. 'I refused because he was too young then. I felt he could wait for another year to play at that level. The next year, I was in charge of the Sikkim team and decided to field him against the heavyweights. He played extremely well along with the senior boys in my team. We beat teams like George Telegraph and Mohammedan Sporting,' he said.

Baichung was slowly blossoming into a fine player. He was razor sharp and could cut through tight defences. After his exploits in the Sikkim Governor's Gold Cup, he would take centre stage when he represented TNA in Subroto Cup in Delhi in 1992.

Delhi witnesses a talent

A soft-spoken and unassuming 16-year-old Baichung hit headlines in the national capital where he shot into the public eye with a first-rate performance. Baichung was declared the best player of the tournament and the media heralded the arrival of a prodigy. He was the charming boy from the hills who immediately caught the attention of a nation whose footballing success was limited to the South Asian Football Federation (SAFF) Cup, a regional tournament where only South Asian teams participate.

'He was shy and soft-spoken. With his red cheeks and smiling face, Baichung was a cute little boy,' said Delhi-based veteran journalist Swapan Sarkar, who covered all the TNA matches in the tournament. 'He was a raw talent. He wasn't a striker then but mostly played as an attacking midfielder,' he recalled.

Sarkar pointed out that like other talented youngsters, he too was lacking in certain basic aspects of the game. 'His distribution was poor, but at that age, he showed signs of a budding star. He mostly played an individual game because he was inexperienced. But later, during his formative years in Calcutta, top coaches such as Syed Nayeemuddin and others ironed out the flaws which helped him a lot,' he explained. 'But it was his knack of scoring goals which attracted me. He was dangerous inside the box and his subtle body movement was amazing,' said Sarkar.

'Bhaskarda (Ganguly), Surajit (Sengupta), and Prasun (Banerjee) were very impressed with Baichung when they watched him play in the Sikkim Governor's Cup. So after the 1992 Subroto Cup, they came to Gangtok in early 1993 and wanted to take him for East Bengal trials. He was sixteen and had already reached his peak in Gangtok, so I thought his next move should be to Calcutta,' Karma said.

In rural Bengal, many such talented youngsters made their way to various clubs in Calcutta through revered coaches and master spotters like Banerjee, Shome, Dukhiram, and Dutta. Samaresh Choudhury was a find of the late Shome while Surajit Sengupta, Prasun Banerjee, Moihul Islam, Sudhir Karmakar were the trainees of the great Achyutda. Achyutda's last product was perhaps the immensely talented Krishanu Dey. After that, there has been none who shone so brilliantly either at the national or at the international level.

I've only heard and read about Achyutda in the various football magazines which were in vogue in Calcutta in the 1970s and 80s. Many top footballers, from P.K. Banerjee to Chuni Goswami, have high regard for the late coach who scouted talent from Bengal's districts and villages.

'He was the guru, the real Dronacharya who did a commendable job by producing so many stars from the grass-roots level,' said Calcutta-based former journalist Ariful Islam.

'Achyutda was known for his relentless and sincere work with the young footballers. He used to train them at the ramparts near the Mohun Bagan ground at the Maidan. Most of his former students like Surajit (Sengupta) and Prasun (Banerjee) helped him with footballs. It's a pity that nobody recognized his devotion. He was a celebrated coach but didn't get any recognition from the government,' he added.

As the legend goes, Prasun, one of India's best midfielders, initially started his career as a striker. He even scored two goals for Khidderpore against East Bengal in the local Calcutta League in 1973 and instantly became famous.

'Achutyda made him play as a midfielder as he thought his left foot was lethal. Prasun even asked his elder brother, P.K. Banerjee, for his suggestions. But P.K. told him that if Achyut sir thought it was better for him to change his position, "I don't have anything to say"', added Islam.

Here I find a striking similarity between Achyutda and Karma. Both knew what suited their wards best; neither of them dreamt of any rewards or awards but maintained a selfless approach towards life and football.

After Achyutda's death, Bengal football was rendered aimless and hopeless. Players were not of the same calibre and standard as they were during the veteran coach's time. The clubs started to bank on outstation talent, but still, none could make a bigger impact than Baichung, whose arrival in Calcutta was like a whiff of fresh air. It was all thanks to Karma who decided to take his protégé to the football capital as he thought it would be the right place for him to unlock his potential.

Tough decision

However, taking Baichung to Calcutta was not an easy decision as the boy was quite young and had been living away from his parents since the age of five. 'I sought the opinion of everybody in Sikkim, but most of them opposed the idea of sending him to Calcutta. I was in a fix. Then I thought that I would listen to my heart and take the risk. I called Baichung's parents over to Gangtok and told them of the situation,' said Karma.

Surprisingly, his parents, who had been reluctant to release him for the sport as a child, wholeheartedly supported the idea as he had already done so well at the junior level in his school and the Boys Club.

'His parents were so simple...and all they said was, "We've no idea about this and since you're taking care of him, you're the best judge". I heaved a sigh of relief. I had been worried that a talent would be wasted had his parents said no to the idea. I took the plunge and brought him to Calcutta,' said Karma.

Before Baichung, only the late Pem Dorjee, who played for India and became the first ever Sikkimese to lead the national team in the early 1980s, had ventured out of his native state. Even before he made his journey, the media was abuzz with the news of his arrival. Baichung's name had spread far and wide and already reached the corridors of most clubs in Calcutta.

'Taking a kid from the hills to the heat of Calcutta was something everyone except his parents was against. Most of them felt the youngster would collapse in the intense heat,' said Karma.

City of Joy

It was a stiflingly hot and sultry June morning in Calcutta in 1993, but Baichung was excited. He was filled with awe, bursting with hope and expectation. He walked through the main entrance and crossed the hallowed gate of one of India's most popular fan-based clubs. The Sikkimese looked at the photographs of players and matches that adorned the walls and felt at peace with the world. He was at the famous East Bengal Club about which he had heard so many fabled stories in his schooldays. His dream had come true and all he wanted was to live up to everybody's expectations.

'It was the peak of summer in Calcutta. I took him to the East Bengal Club for a trial. The first person I met there was Nigerian striker Chima Okorie. His instant reaction was, "Take this boy to Europe and not here," because Chima felt that a boy of Baichung's abilities would do better abroad. But all we could do at that time was put him in the trials at East Bengal. After the trials, I left him with the club and returned to Sikkim, keeping my fingers crossed,' Karma said.

The club was impressed with Baichung and signed him for the 1993–94 season which became a landmark year for both East Bengal and Indian football. With the arrival of the 17-year-old Baichung into the madness of the Calcutta football scene, a new chapter in Indian football began, which would last for the next eighteen years.

However, where Calcutta clubs have boosted the careers of many young players, there also exists a dark side to the opportunities offered. The instant fame has its drawbacks as some of the talented players are drawn into a life of late night parties and other distractions of the city. Partying and drinking into the wee hours means they miss training sessions the next morning. Many a career has been cut short because of this and there are plenty of stories which corroborate it. Before Baichung and even during his career, there have been incidents where young players couldn't handle the fame and fortune they were suddenly bestowed with.

Lalam Puia, much younger than Baichung, played alongside the icon in Mohun Bagan in 2008. Puia was seen as one of the brightest talents after his Tata Football Academy (TFA) days at Jamshedpur. He had tremendous speed and poaching skills which drew comparisons with Baichung. But the diminutive, feisty Puia couldn't handle his drink. He would pick fights and was once arrested after a brawl in a Calcutta hotel only to be bailed out by his club. Later he was sent to a rehab centre. Last heard, the Mizo striker was playing in the low-profile South United Football Club in Bangalore.

Shyamal Ghosh, a former East Bengal player in the 1970s, knew Calcutta inside out and was aware of the depression and frustration the city could foster in vulnerable players. An apprehensive Karma rested easy handing over his best student to Ghosh. After all the hardship Karma went through to bring

Baichung to Calcutta, both of them wanted to make sure that Baichung took the game seriously and avoided distractions. 'Baichung was told to keep away from distractions. He was a good-looking kid who had come to the city from the hills. For a teenager, there was every possibility of getting carried away, but he followed what I told him,' recalled Ghosh.

Baichung remained focussed as he knew that he had left his home far behind to establish himself and had to prove that his initial success with TNA and Boys Club was not a mere flash in the pan.

'Nowadays, young players are only focusssed on the end results and don't make the most of their learning journey,' Karma lamented.

As a player Baichung always had a balanced relationship with the media. He never showed any interest in his own publicity. It was only his performance on the field which was reported, but in a short time, he understood that being carried away by sycophancy and flattery could ruin his career. Instead, he stayed focussed and picked up the nuances of the game which he learnt under different coaches, first at East Bengal and later at Mohun Bagan and Jagatjit Cotton Textiles (JCT) Club.

Much of the credit for Baichung's emergence as an outstanding striker must go to 'Dronacharya' Nayeemuddin who coached him for East Bengal Club in 1995. 'Nayeem sir', as he is known in football circles, nurtured Baichung as only he could, keeping him on the bench and taking him off it at opportune moments. This enabled Baichung to play with a sense of responsibility.

Nayeemuddin was a hard nut to crack, a demanding taskmaster. He was a great trainer, a knowledgeable and wonderful person, but was not one to be easily impressed. Baichung soon realized that there was little sentiment in football, and a club could not maintain the top spot unless there was strong discipline right from the top ranks to the bottom.

When other boys of his age used to go out partying at night, Baichung was single-minded in his desire to be a footballer and avoided most late night get-togethers so that he could attend the morning training. Football always remained his priority.

Baichung's prowess was soon recognized. He had speed, skill, shooting power, strong back-volleys and headers, and a killer instinct inside the penalty box. He was like a hungry hawk that swooped down on the barest of chances and scored.

In the two seasons he spent at East Bengal Club, he gained a lot of confidence and his career took off in a big way. Media attention could have made a young lad cocky, but Karma's down-to-earth realism was ingrained in him. He kept his feet firmly on the ground.

I asked Baichung if, while leaving Tinkitam, he had ever thought that he would become the face of Indian football.

'I just wanted to be a good footballer. I dreamt of wearing the national jersey one day, but I was not very ambitious. It was only after 1997 that I felt I was making a name for myself,' said Baichung.

Maiden strike

Ghosh gave Baichung his first break when he brought him in as a substitute in a match against Bangladesh's Brothers Union in the All Airlines Gold Cup 1993 in his first year. He donned the bright red and yellow colours, laced his boots, and was soon in his element. He stamped his entry with a goal in East Bengal's 6–0 win. From that day on, he immersed himself in his new role as a poacher.

Baichung's spectacular back-volley in the Durand Cup that year in Delhi is still remembered by those who watched him at the packed Ambedkar Stadium. Old-timers compared Baichung's goal, which took the red-and-gold brigade to the final, to Shyam Thapa's effort for Mohun Bagan against Mafatlals in the same tournament in 1978.

'He scored some fascinating goals and from great angles. What made him a great striker was that he knew the art of scoring goals and that's what matters in football,' Jo Paul Ancheri said about Baichung.

Baichung was heralded as a star. So much so that celebrated cartoonist R.K. Laxman featured Baichung in one of his art works with the caption 'Boy, Oh Boy'. Former Indian goalkeeper Tanumoy Basu who was Baichung's teammate in East Bengal in 1993 recalled an incident that convinced him about Baichung's poaching skills.

'In the 1994 Santosh Trophy final against Punjab in Chennai, one of Baichung's crosses from the right wing earned us a goal and later he scored a golden goal to win the title for Bengal,' said Tanumoy.

In his first season, Baichung wanted to ensure that he also continued his studies and hence enrolled in a correspondence course at the Assembly of God Church School in Park Street. He couldn't complete Class XII despite taking admission in a higher secondary school at Dum Dum near Calcutta as he got busier and busier with football.

'I've known him since his early days when I was a cadet at TFA and he was playing for TNA. He was a very serious player on the field, but a complete prankster off it. We had some great times playing for the national team and the club,' said Renedy Singh, one of his closest friends in the national team.

When news about him reached other parts of the country, many clubs were keen to sign him. They were convinced that he was a star in the making and were ready to pay any price to have Baichung in their team. But Baichung's heart and mind stayed with East Bengal in the first two seasons before he left the city to join the now defunct JCT team, Punjab, which won the first National Football League (NFL) in 1996 when Baichung joined.

'Baichung was an interesting youngster who had a passion for scoring goals. He was friendly towards foreigners and gelled well with outstation players,' said former Nigerian striker Stephen Abarowei, his teammate at the Punjab club.

Baichung walked away with the best player and highest goal-scorer awards to establish himself as one of the deadliest strikers in Indian football.

'His decision to join the star-studded JCT in 1996 was a good one as he became the top scorer with fourteen goals,' said former India midfielder Tejinder Kumar, who first met him at the SAI Centre in Calcutta in 1992 when he was an under-16 player.

P.K. Banerjee said that Baichung was one of the most superior talents that he had come across in his career as a coach with both East Bengal and Mohun Bagan. 'When I was the TFA director it was just unfortunate that I couldn't bring him there. But later when he came to Calcutta, he played under my coaching. I still remember his first hat-trick against Bagan in 1997 when East Bengal won 4–1. It announced his arrival,' said the legend. 'He was in the last batch that I coached in East Bengal and he was amazing right from day one.'

Karma too believed that his ward was special; he had the attitude and maturity to cope with the mental strain of the game, something many other talented players could not do.

MBA Rendezvous, a preparatory training institute for aspiring students in Delhi, mentions Baichung in one of their motivational stories to students, 'Success is not instant. It takes years of patience, diligence and determination, and this is what we can learn from Baichung.'

But looking back, the former Boys Club coach lamented that some of Baichung's abilities were underutilized and his potential was never fully realized. 'There were many plus points in his game. He had excellent headers which most coaches didn't utilize as he never got accurate crosses from his teammates. Whenever I went to Calcutta I used to tell the coaches to make good use of his headers, but they ignored me,' said Karma, who retired as sports secretary in the Sikkim government last year.

'If he were in Europe, or anywhere abroad for that matter, his training and strengthening would have been different and he could have gone to another level as Chima had once told me,' he added.

In his first ever international outing in a Nehru Cup match in 1995, Baichung came in as a substitute for his idol I.M. Vijayan against Thailand.

'He's like my younger brother. I was senior to him, but we didn't have that senior–junior relationship. I think we played more than twenty international matches together. As a young player he was too good,' said Vijayan, who played for several top clubs in India, including JCT, where he played alongside the young Baichung.

'Baichung was a great fan of Vijayan who, in turn, said that Baichung was the biggest star in the making,' added Karma.

In the next match against Uzbekistan in Calcutta, Baichung shone again. He became India's youngest scorer at nineteen in the team's surprise 1–0 win against the then Asian Games champions Uzbekistan at the Salt Lake Stadium in Calcutta. After parading his skills at the Nehru Cup, Baichung mesmerized fans in Colombo's Sugathadasa Stadium at the SAARC Gold Cup in 1995. His flying header against the hosts was hailed by experts as one of the best goals scored by an Indian striker in an international tournament. Besides, his captivating performances at home in the Federation Cup and Santosh Trophy saw his popularity sky-rocket.

Just three years after his debut for India, his talent was acknowledged by the Indian government when he was conferred the Arjuna Award. When he completed 100 matches for the country, playing against Turkmenistan in the 2009 Nehru Cup, Baichung got the nation's second-highest civilian award, the Padma Shri.

'He was very agile near the goal. In a short time, he emerged as a mature striker,' said Tejinder, his senior teammate in the national team.

Karma was aware that one of Baichung's greatest strengths was consistency which was crucial for survival in the cut-throat competitiveness of the Indian clubs. According to his mentor, Baichung also had a calculated approach. But commenting on his drawbacks, Karma observed that though he had a very good temperament, at times he seemed to lose his cool over referees' decisions. No wonder then that he received marching orders during crunch games. 'That was the one area which I always told him to work on,' said Karma.

Though Karma didn't say it in so many words, he mentioned that sometimes a player tends to become a little self-centred when he is trying to prove himself.

'I remember telling Baichung and Mohun Bagan's Brazilian striker Ramirez Barreto to complement each other when they played together. I guess in an atmosphere of stiff competition when two top strikers play together, selfishness is bound to creep in,' he explained.

On the other hand, the Brazilian has been quite a buddy to Baichung. Both of them led Bagan's attack and though successes were few, those which came were stamped with the superior performance of the duo. 'Baichung was more than the face of Indian football. He was an inspirational footballer who was focussed and played with tenacity,' said Barreto.

'Correct your mistakes and work on your technique, and you'll not keep repeating them. Remember, a man who never makes mistakes, never gets anywhere. Have you got that, son?' Karma had once told his favourite protégé. Baichung's keenness to learn from and improve on his mistakes was, in fact, what made him a star.

I find it perplexing and unfortunate that Karma missed out on the Dronacharya Award when almost every guru from Ramakant Achrekar in cricket to O.M. Nambiar in athletics has been felicitated with it. Perhaps his work didn't receive enough endorsement from the people who held power. Looking back, Baichung's 60-year-old soft-spoken Karma 'uncle', however, is happy and contented that he could contribute to the growth of Indian football.

After his favourite student bid adieu to the game in 2011, Karma attributed his success to determination and commitment. 'He is Indian football's role model. He always has this positive attitude towards everything in life. He was hardworking for sure, but it was his selfless approach to the game which made him a star. All young and aspiring footballers can look up to him,' said the man who will always be remembered for the great contribution he made to Indian football.

As Calvin said in his book, Karma will remain the ubiquitous yet anonymous member of football's hidden tribe.

3

Route to East Bengal

In 1981, when I was a precocious 10-year-old football fanatic, I had the opportunity to watch former India captain and goalkeeper Bhaskar Ganguly in a live match between Mohammedan Sporting and Aryans at the Mohun Bagan ground. Bhaskar was the country's best keeper at the time and captained the Indian team in the 1982 Asian Cup.

During my last visit to India in July 2013, I met Bhaskar in his State Bank of India office at its Ultadanga branch in east Calcutta exactly thirty-two years after I had first seen him on a football pitch. I wanted to glean his thoughts on the Baichung phenomenon. Now middle-aged with a paunch and suffering from Parkinson's disease, the former star is not media-savvy and stays away from the limelight. He does not talk much about football and seldom visits the Maidan where many footballers of Calcutta, like himself, played for glory. Even a Google search yields surprisingly scant information about this former star. Current football journalists, too, have not written much about him.

When I met him, Bhaskar was dressed casually in a light pink T-shirt and trousers, staying true to his preference for keeping things simple and low-key.

'*Cholo bhai, neecher floor e jai, ekhane sobai ektu byasto ache, disturb hote pare* (Brother, let's go down to the floor below. Here, my colleagues are busy and they might get disturbed),' he said.

I followed him to the bank's second floor where he found a quiet corner.

'*Du cup cha diye ja* (Give us two cups of tea),' he told one of the canteen boys.

He didn't seem to be too interested in discussing the game's progress in the country. But when I asked him about Baichung, his eyes lit up with excitement.

'Oh, Baichung, he was a wonderful boy,' he exclaimed.

Bhaskar then narrated the story of how he discovered Baichung at a football camp conducted at Paljor Stadium in Gangtok in 1992.

'We were in Sikkim for the Sikkim Governor's Gold Cup. At the same time, SBI wanted to host a football clinic for youngsters in Gangtok. I, along with my footballer friend and SBI colleague Surajit Sengupta, was asked to organize it. A lot of young Sikkimese boys enthusiastically joined the camp and the response was tremendous,' he said. 'At the camp, we noticed one boy who was really passionate about the game. He was very sharp and his shooting skills were amazing. He impressed both of us. My sixth sense told me that this guy was a bundle of talent.

'I asked him his name. He said "Baichung". When I asked him if he wanted to play in Calcutta for East Bengal, he pointed to his mentor, Karma (Bhutia). We asked Karma to contact us in Calcutta,' Bhaskar said.

'Baichung was very shy and didn't speak much. Initially, even his parents didn't like the idea of sending their young son to Calcutta as they were more interested in his studies. But, finally, Karma succeeded in convincing Baichung's parents that he would take care of his studies as well,' he added.

That is how young Baichung started his journey from Tinkitam to Gangtok and then to Calcutta.

'Paltuda, who was then the East Bengal secretary, was convinced when I told him about Baichung. So, that's how it all started. There was another talented boy in the camp with him—Sherap. He too had great skill, but his parents didn't allow him to go to Calcutta,' Bhaskar said.

At times, I wonder how things would have been if Baichung had not turned up at that camp, or if Bhaskar had not noticed his talent, or Baichung's parents had not allowed him to go to Calcutta. One thing is for certain—Indian football wouldn't have been the same. Bhaskar's contribution to Indian football has been considerable, but his discovery and induction of the Sikkimese Sniper into mainstream football will be remembered with special gratitude.

Old-timers say that in 1965, when youngsters Mohammed Habib and Syed Nayeemuddin joined the red-and-gold brigade, there was always a mad rush to watch the two talented Hyderabadis play. In 1993, Baichung, with his innocuous baby face, was greeted with a similar wave of love and affection, and he soon became the darling of football aficionados in the city.

'There was an air of class about him, something not associated with a footballer,' said former journalist Sujit Bhar who interviewed a young Baichung in 1993.

Baichung took to Calcutta like a fish to water.

'Initially, I felt a bit lonely, but gradually I overcame it. After all, I had spent most of my student life in a hostel, away from my family. Calcutta was not new to me as I had been to the city before I joined East Bengal,' said Baichung.

'When I was a student, I knew very little about Indian football and had only heard about East Bengal and Mohun Bagan when they played in Sikkim. It was only in 1993, when East Bengal offered me to join, that I started to take it all seriously,' Baichung said about his introduction to one of India's premier clubs, formed in 1920.

When he first donned the East Bengal jersey, he was paid Rs 50,000 per season. The following season in 1994, the figure rose to between Rs 1.5 lakh and Rs 2 lakh. In 1995, when everybody realized his potential, he became the highest paid player in the club at Rs 5 lakh per season.

Baichung was an amateur player when he came to the city. He had no idea about the stiff competition, the pressure and the over-exhaustion that many young players faced once they joined the top Calcutta teams. But he was fortunate—after Karma brought the 17-year-old to the city, he was treated with care and consideration by the club. During his initial months, everyone ensured that he was not overly exposed or stressed out as a player.

'I must thank coach Shyamal Ghosh who took great care of him in his maiden season at East Bengal. He used him intelligently, initially as a substitute, and encouraged him to learn the nuances of club football,' said Bhaskar.

Ghosh did handle Baichung well—he did not immediately throw the young player into the competition. In fact, had it not been for Ghosh, Baichung might well have become one of the many promising young talents who fade into oblivion during their formative years in Calcutta football.

'I was looking for a young player as I was preparing a junior East Bengal squad. Bhaskar told me that there was a youngster from Sikkim and that I must have a look at him. After watching him in the trials, I immediately felt that this boy had something in him,' said 63-year-old Ghosh, who now holds training sessions for juniors at an academy based in Ultadanga.

'He was good in the air besides having good skills. So he impressed me quickly. His mentor, Karma, had told me that I should take note of Baichung's header. Karma was right—Baichung's headers were so good that they reminded me of Shyam Thapa,' added the former East Bengal coach.

Ghosh couldn't have asked for more as the Sikkimese showed immense maturity in his first major break as a substitute for 45 minutes against Bangladesh's Brothers Union in an All Airlines Gold Cup match on 2 April 1993.

Maiden hat-trick

Baichung announced his arrival with a maiden goal in his team's 6–0 win. His first recorded hat-trick for East Bengal was against George Telegraph in a Super Division Calcutta League match on 28 June, 1994.

'He was very young at the time. I wanted to protect him from undue pressure which is quite common when someone this young turns up to play for a big club like East Bengal. I used him sparingly by sending him as a substitute,' said Ghosh.

Baichung had a tumultuous love affair with East Bengal. Though he played for JCT, Bury FC, and Mohun Bagan during his career, which started with East Bengal in 1993, he donned the red-and-yellow shirt for the last time in his career in 2009. In the four phases when he played for East Bengal, from 1993–95, 1997–99, 2003–05 and 2009, Baichung was central to many of the club's triumphs, which also included one of their famous victories abroad—the ASEAN Cup in Jakarta in 2003.

'I've received a lot of love from everyone in this club. I can never forget the contribution of Shankar mali, the veteran groundsman of the club,' said Baichung, who played 317 matches for the red-and-gold team.

Shankar Pillai had come to Calcutta from Tamil Nadu in the 1940s and spent his entire life with East Bengal. With his intricate understanding of the nature of the ground he maintained, he was a guide to many footballers who came from outside Calcutta, including Baichung. Shankar died in 2002 at the age of seventy-eight, after serving the club for almost half a century.

'He was such a great help,' Baichung said. 'He would often tell me what boots to wear in different weather conditions, and on slushy and hard grounds. I believe that he was one of the people who helped me grow as a top footballer in Calcutta,' he added.

Baichung left East Bengal for the first time in the 1995–96 season for JCT, a club based in Phagwara, Punjab.

'Actually, I didn't want to be known as an out-and-out East Bengal player. I love the club and their fans. But I also wanted to play for other Indian clubs,' he said.

This was an honest admission by Baichung and he openly told East Bengal officials that he wanted to play for other clubs as well. After two seasons with East Bengal, he moved north, and it was JCT, now a disbanded club, who were privileged to have the super talent. They were once a leading team from north India who won their maiden and only NFL title in 1996–97 thanks to Baichung's amazing form. He scored fourteen goals that heralded his arrival on the national scene.

Tejinder Kumar, Baichung's teammate at JCT, felt that it was the right decision for a youngster like him to play away from the media glare in Calcutta.

'At JCT the pressure and expectations from the club and fans were much less than in Calcutta. Hence, for a youngster like him the decision to play there was a good one. He could devote more time to the game,' he said.

Tejinder's observation proved correct. Baichung's value soared in the transfer market. In four years' time, he was widely regarded as the star player in Indian football and every club wanted to sign him on.

'After our first interaction during a SAI tournament in Delhi in 1991—he represented Tashi Namgyal Academy and I, Tata Football Academy—we met again at East Bengal six years later.

'It was the best time of our lives. Baichung, Soso, Ajay Singh and I formed the core of the team under PK sir. We had a great season that year,' reminisced Renedy.

'Chung Chung' cuts Dutta's Diamond to pieces

Once again he returned to the city where it had all begun—Calcutta. The 1997–98 season with East Bengal turned out to be one of Baichung's best with the club. He had matured as a striker and was in devastating form. In his new avatar in Indian football, Baichung showed just how lethal he could be as a striker. His super hat-trick against Mohun Bagan in the 1997 Federation Cup semifinal still rankles Bagan coach Amal Dutta and fans of the club.

A Bagan–East Bengal derby has a striking similarity to the Scottish Premier League's Old Firm derby between Rangers and Celtic, since a majority of Bagan fans represent the 'nativist' population and East Bengal fans represent the 'immigrants'.

Dutta, one of India's most tactically sound coaches during his time, paid the price for his silly 'Chung Chung' remark about the young Baichung on the eve of the semifinal. Dutta had to eat his words when the striker demolished Bagan with a record hat-trick in East Bengal's 4–1 historic win at the packed Salt Lake Stadium in Calcutta on 13 July, 1997. That derby established Baichung's superstardom as he cut to pieces Dutta's much-touted 'Diamond System'.

While he established himself at East Bengal, his school back in Gangtok kept everyone in the loop about its famous student's exploits in Calcutta through newspaper clippings on the notice board.

'But the clippings got fewer once he became a star because every student at TNA or, for that matter, the whole of Sikkim was aware of Agya's achievements. Simply put, he became a star and the paper cuttings on the notice board were not needed any more,' said Saurabh Chamling, Baichung's junior in school.

During that crucial semifinal, Bagan earned seven corners in the first 25 minutes, but somehow still managed to fluff their chances. After the first half hour, Bagan began to show signs of fatigue owing to the humid July weather in Calcutta. Dutta's opposite number in East Bengal, P.K. Banerjee, was waiting for this opportunity. He played a master stroke by deploying Baichung towards the flanks and young Nazim-ul Haq as the centre-forward.

P.K. knew Baichung's strength was his sudden burst of speed, and instructed him to exploit the empty space behind Bagan's central defenders Ranjan Dey and James Odiambo who went high up the pitch for their counter-attacks. It was Bagan that dominated in the first quarter but East Bengal shocked them with a goal from a counter-attack when Haq scored a thumping side-volley with a left-footer in the 25th minute after the Bagan defence failed to clear a corner from Soso. After half-time, East Bengal doubled their lead as Baichung leapt brilliantly to connect a header from another Soso corner.

'Soso and I had practised corners for a long time. He used to keep it in the first bar and I had to come from behind and head it home,' he said about his first goal in the match that saw a record footfall at the Salt Lake Stadium. In the presence of 1,31,000 fans, an Asian record that holds till date, it was an opportune moment for him to shine.

By this time Bagan were desperate for an equalizer, though their forays no longer had the same sting. Their Nigerian striker Chima Okorie managed to shake off the Kenyan Sammy Omollo and pulled one back from close in the 66th minute, but Bagan's jubilation ended shortly after Baichung took centre stage once again.

Baichung's pyrotechnics were noted and hailed as something that had not been seen in Indian football for many years. Dutta's pre-match comments may have spurred young Baichung to take his performance a notch higher against East Bengal's traditional rivals. 'His spot jumps were phenomenal and he could use both legs. He was a great finisher,' said Chima.

He exploited Bagan's poor positioning of full-backs in the defence. Sharp and agile, Baichung broke the offside trap time and again, speeding past his markers. His second goal came after a typically shambolic defence from Bagan as he dribbled past goalkeeper Hemanta Dora to hit the ball right into the top corner of the net in the 85th minute.

P.K. believed Baichung had that much-needed fire within him which helped him to carve a niche for himself.

'He is always dangerous inside the box. Before the match I only advised him to play his normal game and make it a point to remain as far as possible near the Bagan box, which he did,' said the former coach.

Three minutes later, he dashed inside the box; East Bengal debutant Shamsy Reza released a pass to Baichung, who then wanted to pass it to Haq. But the ball was intercepted by a Bagan defender who, however, failed to control it and Baichung tapped it home for a well-deserved hat-trick, the first in the derby's seventy-two-year history!

In the twilight of his coaching career, Dutta's conception of the 'Diamond System' for Bagan in 1997 made him famous. He earned a name for being an innovative thinker of formations and football ideologies. Interestingly, he could explain his socialist thinking using the language of football.

The veteran coach used a three-back system in his celebrated Diamond 3-4-3 formation where the width in the team had to come from the full-backs pushing forward. The defensive midfielder was sometimes used as a deep-lying playmaker.

Dutta's new formation was designed to extract the best performance from his players. Innovations were his hallmark and he never shied away from experimentation as he never wanted his teams to play tedious drawn games. In his own words, 'The beautiful game must look attractive and beautiful.' He always wanted Indian football to stay in sync with modern tactics and styles.

'For me, a football team is like a society. Everyone must contribute to its development. Hence, the Diamond System which I used in Bagan was aimed at utilizing each and every player when they attacked,' explained Dutta.

That humiliating defeat against East Bengal is still fresh in Dutta's mind. The veteran coach who is now in his eighties still remembers every bit of the game—Bagan's slothful defence and how Baichung made a mockery of his Diamond System. But surprisingly, Dutta still refused to acknowledge Baichung's greatness as a player.

Sixteen years after that game, in August 2013, solely for the purpose of this book and also to do justice to Baichung, I decided to meet Dutta. I wanted to understand why he, one of India's most technically sound coaches, had ridiculed Baichung by calling him 'Chung Chung' in a controversial pre-match interview.

'Can I come and meet him?' I asked his wife on the phone.

'Yes, you can, but come before lunch as he is particular about timings,' she said.

Teghoria is only a 30-minute drive from Phoolbagan on the eastern fringes of Calcutta, but anticipating traffic owing to construction work for the metro rail on the Eastern Bypass, I left early. It was cloudy; the occasional drizzle had given some respite to the city after a stifling sudorific spell.

At the Phoolbagan crossing, I hailed one of Calcutta's famous all-yellow taxis, whose speed can be best described as stately. I was meeting Dutta for the first time after 2003 when he used to coach the United Sports Club, then known as Eveready FC. I have a sincere regard for him and always found him to be a genuine and well-read man with sound theoretical knowledge of the game. I didn't want to profile him as there was already enough newsprint on the Euclid of Indian football.

As the taxi moved at a snail's pace, I tried to recollect the first time I saw him. I remembered a poster of his in a 1980 football magazine, when he had been the coach of Mohammedan Sporting. Then in his fifties, the picture depicted him with a whistle between his lips and one arm raised, probably instructing players during a training session.

Despite his retirement from coaching, Dutta is immensely popular. From West Bengal's Chief Minister Mamata Banerjee to his neighbourhood club, everybody still invites him to attend various football programmes and seminars. Unable to locate his house once the cab entered a narrow lane off Baguihati near Teghoria, I kept asking the passers-by and roadside vendors about India's first professional coach.

'Go a little farther, you'll find his home just opposite a football ground,' said one shop-owner. But on reaching a serpentine lane a kilometre away from his house, the driver parked the iconic Ambassador near a roadside tea stall with a grim face.

'*Sahab, yeh taxi aage nahin ja sakti hai. Aage wale tyre mein shayad puncture hai* (Sir, this taxi cannot go any farther. One of its front tyres seems to be punctured),' he said. But a couple of middle-aged men at the tea stall advised me to take a cycle rickshaw to his house, which was just a stone's throw away. And there it was, on the right side of a narrow stretch—house no. T-85, Rajarhat Road, Baguihati—Dutta's 30-year-old two-storey house, built when he had been India's leading coach. It resembled his person—simple and unpretentious.

In the drawing room, I found Dutta resting on a sofa. On the side table, there were a couple of unfolded Bengali newspapers and a thick *Rabindra Rachanabali,* a collection of Tagore's writings. It seemed that Dutta, a voracious reader, had just finished reading them.

He rose to meet me and we entered into an impromptu discussion on the game. In the course of our chat, I told him that I still have a letter he wrote to me in 2002, thanking me for sending him a copy of his interview.

I found that even at eighty-three, Dutta was up to talking about anything from Tagore to the dwindling standard of football in the state and in India.

Dutta was born in 1920 to a family that stayed right opposite Tagore's iconic house at Jorasanko in north Calcutta.

A competent midfielder with East Bengal in the 1950s, Dutta represented India in the 1954 Asian Games at Manila. After his playing career was over, he went to England for a year-long FA coaching course, where he was taught by the renowned Walter Winterbottom.

'The entrance test was difficult as I had to go through a set of physiology questions. Thankfully, I was a student of physiology and it helped in the end.

'Football is not only about the game. You need to understand the human body—the joints, the cartilages, the heart and liver, the kidney functions,' he explained.

An innovative coach—famed for his football philosophy that many felt was ahead of his time—Dutta was recognized as the finest thinker of the game in India.

In the early 1960s, he quit Indian Railways to become a full-time coach. Knowing that he had never admired Baichung, I avoided mentioning him right at the start. Instead, we spoke about the first time he saw his illustrious neighbour, Rabindranath Tagore, from his ancestral house.

'I used to see him keeping an eye on us from his balcony while we made frantic efforts to use their open space for football,' he said, recalling his childhood days at Jorasanko.

As I sat listening to his experiences, a middle-aged autorickshaw driver entered the room. *'Amalda, goto koek din jabot amar dan hantu te prochondo byatha* (Amalda, my right knee has been hurting badly these last few days),' he said.

Dutta, who had also chipped in as a part-time physician, touched his knee and nodded his head.

'There's a jerk in the inner cartilage, but it's nothing to worry about. Do the cold-and-hot-water treatment and use a kneecap when you drive the autorickshaw. *Ami ekta tablet likhe dichhi, oshudher dokan theke kine niyo* (I am prescribing a medicine, get it from the chemist's).'

I wondered if this was a missed opportunity for Indian football. Why wasn't his vast knowledge of physiology and football utilized better?

Slowly steering the conversation to football once he was fully engaged, I asked him whether he thought Baichung was one of the greatest Indian footballers.

'No, no. He was an average footballer,' he said sharply.

I replied with another question: If Baichung was an average player, how did he score a hat-trick and bamboozle Bagan, the team which Dutta had coached in 1997? The veteran coach paused, smiled and ran his fingers through his hair. He had an answer, but couldn't put it into words. 'Intelligent' was the only word he could come up with.

Both in the clubs and in the national team, Baichung had to work his way towards the goal and find gaps in the rival defence. His exuberance and high fitness level were spectacular and appreciated by all coaches, including his sharpest critic and former national coach, Syed Nayeemuddin.

'He knew when to shine and how to do his job well. The good thing about him was that he knew how to spend less energy and maximize the effort, which ensured that he wouldn't get tired easily,' said Shamsy, who played alongside Baichung in the national team during the 1998 Bangkok Asian Games.

Nayeemuddin always appreciated Baichung's fitness and agility in the early years, but once relations soured, the veteran coach made it a habit to criticize him. But like Nayeemuddin, Dutta too refused to accept his greatness as a player.

Offer from Singapore

Regardless of such criticism, Baichung was chased by clubs both in India and abroad.

'I tried to sign Baichung for Home United in 2005. This was based purely on his ability as a player as he had been recommended to me by a few people whose opinion I respected. I watched videos of him and offered him a contract,' said former Home United manager Steve Darby.

'He came to Singapore and we met. Eventually, we couldn't agree on the terms as Home United had a strict salary cap. But all the negotiations were done in such a professional and honest manner that it was a pleasure dealing with him. I had no idea of his popularity then—I just wanted him because he was a good player,' said Darby.

There were plenty of offers from other clubs too. Dempo Sports Club and Churchill Brothers, both based in Goa, wanted to sign him on. But he declined their offers as he preferred to stay in Calcutta. He loved the atmosphere of the city and its proximity to Sikkim was an added advantage. Baichung had another reason to refuse offers from the Goan clubs.

'I always wanted to play in clubs with good infrastructure. Goan clubs don't have it but Calcutta clubs at least have their own grounds,' he explained.

India's first professional club, FC Kochin, too, was keen to have him on their side. Formed in 1996 by a group of Malayali businessmen and NRIs with a capital of Rs 1 crore, and managed by Babu Mather, a former sports writer for a Gulf daily, FC Kochin was unique. The club's motto was 'A new approach to the game'.

'We wanted Baichung in the 1998–99 season, but FC Kochin could not afford him. And at that time, I.M. Vijayan, Raman Vijayan, Jo Paul Ancheri, Carlton Chapman and four Nigerians were already with us—they were all highly rated players. Baichung was having a successful season with East Bengal and getting him on board would have been the icing on the cake,' said Babu.

After Baichung was released by Bury FC in England in 2002, he did not join any club immediately, preferring to weigh his options instead. Though East Bengal wanted him, he remained surprisingly quiet about his next move. His decision, however, would disappoint East Bengal fans. Many hearts were broken as he accepted an offer from Bagan. It was difficult for East Bengal fans to accept that their favourite player had joined their perennial foe.

'East Bengal and Bagan are the two biggest clubs in Calcutta. Obviously, I wanted to wear the Bagan colours too. It was not that I didn't like the atmosphere at East Bengal,' Baichung said.

However, his stint with Bagan turned out to be a major disappointment. He was injured early on and failed to play again that season, missing Bagan's only trophy win—the All Airlines Gold Cup.

In the football city, people still weave tales of East Bengal fans using black magic to stop Baichung from performing for Bagan. However, Baichung himself admits that his first season with Bagan was far from impressive as his injury troubled him relentlessly.

Nowhere near his best with Bagan, which he joined for the first time in 2002–03 after his stint in Bury, Baichung may have realized that he could have performed better in his favourite club, East Bengal, after all.

During 2002–03, Bagan's club politics took the sheen off the team's performance. Football was pushed to the back-burner as the club officials fought a nasty court battle for control of the club's administration. Their star players, including Barreto—Baichung's striking partner—lost interest and quit the club a year later. Baichung was left confused.

During one of my meetings with him at the Bagan club lawn in April 2003, Baichung revealed his displeasure. He was visibly upset. His injury aside, the atmosphere in the club was not ideal for a professional player like him. Baichung's heart and soul had remained with East Bengal, but contractual obligations would not allow him to switch over to East Bengal midway during the season. He had no choice but to wait for the season to end.

In the 2003–04 season, Baichung was back in East Bengal. He looked happy and contented when he signed on the dotted line at the International Football Association (IFA), Bengal football's parent body. There was posse of television reporters waiting for him outside the IFA. Baichung obliged everyone with quick interviews before he got into the car and headed for Hyatt Regency where the East Bengal team was staying.

This was undoubtedly one of his best years with the club. His presence added strength and punch to a team coached by the maverick Subhash Bhowmick, another stalwart who had always held Baichung in high esteem. East Bengal's biggest international success that year was the ASEAN Cup win. Baichung scored a goal in East Bengal's 3–1 win over BEC Tero Sasana, and was named the man of the match. He also scored in the 1–1 draw against Petrokimia Putra and scored five goals in a 6–0 win against Philippine Army FC in the group stages. When the championship ended, he finished as the top scorer with nine goals to his name.

'He liked East Bengal and their fans very much,' said Sherap, who also played in the same club in 1997.

Back home, Baichung guided East Bengal to win NFL and became the highest scorer with twelve goals. In the next season, he hit the net nine times as East Bengal finished third in the League. His brilliant form continued in the 2005–06 season when he scored another dozen goals to earn the All India Football Federation (AIFF) Player of the Year award.

There was indeed a peculiar chemistry between him and the club. Whenever he donned the red and yellow colours, he shone. He was razor sharp as a striker and hit top form. The flame never burnt out.

He had always had good relations with East Bengal, but there was also a moment when he was upset with the club officials. If in 2003, he left Bagan because he was harried and wanted to return 'home' to East Bengal, three years later he was disheartened on account of payment issues. He didn't want to renew his contract with East Bengal which ended in 2006–07.

For the first time, he left the club deeply hurt.

'I had to wait too long for my dues. The club tested my patience. Because of injuries, I even offered a 20 per cent cut subject to certain promises but they failed even on that count,' revealed Baichung. It was the first time that differences had cropped up between him and his once-favourite club.

Though the bridges weren't burnt, he left the club in the new season for his second stint with Bagan in 2006–07. This stint was also low-key. Something kept stopping him from hitting the net, and his indifferent form became the talk of the town. Only once in the Super Cup in Gurgaon did he dazzle with a hat-trick as Bagan beat I-League champions Dempo Sports Club 5–0.

At Gurgaon, finally, he felt satisfied after regaining both his confidence and his form. There was a glint in his eye that May afternoon even though he had rediscovered himself a trifle too late in the hectic season. But he made use of that season-ending Cup to ensure that his popularity graph remained intact despite a none-too-impressive season with the green-and-maroon brigade.

Such was his emotional bond with East Bengal that he wanted to return to the club after a bitter fight with their traditional rivals, Bagan, in 2009, following his participation in the dance reality show, *Jhalak Dikhhla Jaa*.

On 22 June, 2009, when the former India skipper officially signed with East Bengal for the fourth time in his career on a one-year contract, Bagan stepped in to stop the move. Things turned ugly as Bagan claimed that he was contractually bound to stay with them for another year and thus could not sign with East Bengal. Baichung's lawyer, Usha Nath Banerjee, in his petition said that a player above twenty-eight years of age was free to make a choice of club in the third year of his contract.

Baichung declared this contract with East Bengal as his homecoming.

'This is the club from where it all started and it is here that I'll end my club career,' said Baichung after he was cleared to play for East Bengal in 2009.

Though Bagan did its best to stop Baichung's switchover to East Bengal, he was allowed to don the East Bengal colours one last time by the AIFF-appointed arbitrator, Amarendra Sharan, former additional solicitor general of India.

The mercurial striker missed most of the 2009–10 season because of his national team duties. It was also a season when he was plagued by injuries. But he promised to quit as an East Bengal player, which he did before joining his own club, United Sikkim, in 2011. On his love–hate relationship with both the clubs, he says, 'Despite the shortcomings in both these clubs, we must appreciate their work. I think even the best of clubs like Manchester United or Arsenal wouldn't have survived, had they been based in India.'

4

A Traitor?

Syed Nayeemuddin took out a clipping of a Bangladeshi newspaper from his travel-worn suitcase in his hotel room at Delhi's Le Meridien, where I was meeting him for an interview. 'See this. See how much love and respect I've got from them after becoming their national coach,' said India's once most decorated football coach. He was then guiding the Bangladesh football team in the 2007 Nehru Cup—the first Indian to coach a foreign national team.

Nayeem, who is now coaching the Bangladeshi club Brothers Union in Dhaka, is a former great, once hailed as India's best defender. A true Dronacharya, his coaching skills were recognized when he led Mohun Bagan and East Bengal in the early 1990s and various Indian teams until 2006. He is considered as one of the best coaches after P.K. Banerjee who scooped up a bagful of trophies with the two top clubs in

Calcutta. He hails from Hyderabad, but has made Calcutta his home since 1966, when he came to the city as an East Bengal player.

Over the years, since meeting him for the first time during the 1997 Durand Cup in Delhi, I have had the opportunity to interview him many times. However, no matter how many times we meet and what else we talk about, Nayeem invariably arrives at his favourite topic—Baichung Bhutia. The coach never misses a chance to remind others of the fact that he is not particularly fond of Baichung.

I have tried, on many occasions, to understand his grouse against Baichung. Nayeem has never really chucked his football boot at Baichung, unlike the furious Alex Ferguson who chucked his at David Beckham after Manchester United's loss to Arsenal at Old Trafford in 2003. But Baichung has always found himself at the receiving end of Nayeem's rant, not only during his entire coaching career but even today.

Ironically, it was Nayeem who, as the East Bengal coach in 1995, had guided the young Baichung in Calcutta. The 70-year-old has been instrumental in shaping the career of many footballers and Baichung is one of them. Nayeem had been by his side like a protective father and never burdened the young player with impossible expectations. It was he who had suggested that Baichung begin as an attacking midfielder rather than an out-and-out striker. The veteran coach even compared his skills with those of Japan's former international Hidetoshi Nakata and always maintained that Baichung could have reached far greater heights. Once he gauged Baichung's talent, he wanted to safeguard the kid from the glare of the media. This was acceptable to a certain extent, but the coach's efforts to keep the footballer caged within the boundaries of his own philosophy and preoccupations soon became torturous for the young Baichung. But Nayeem's idea bore fruit in later years, for Baichung sharpened his skills as a poacher while he played behind the main striker. Baichung, however, gives all the credit for this to former national coach Rustam Akhramov from Uzbekistan, under whom he made his India debut in 1995.

Clash of the titans

Things went from bad to worse between coach and player, but no one knows for sure what triggered this disharmony between the two. Maybe it was Nayeem's overprotective and imposing nature that didn't go down well with some of the players, including Baichung.

Nayeem also didn't like Baichung's friendship with former East Bengal teammate Soso, with whom the player shared a flat in his early years in Calcutta. Nayeem felt that Soso's 'wayward' lifestyle would affect young Baichung's career. The former Manipuri player was never in Nayeem's good books and was omitted from the national team which played in the 1997 SAFF Cup in Kathmandu, Nepal. The decision that left his friend out of the team may also have tarnished their relationship.

The first reports of a feud between the two popular names in Indian football surfaced during the 1998 Asian Games held in

Bangkok, when India lost 1–0 to Japan in a preliminary group match. At twenty-two, Baichung was already a star, especially after his breathtaking hat-trick for East Bengal against Mohun Bagan in the historic Federation Cup semifinal in Calcutta in July 1997. As Baichung's popularity soared, the coach distanced himself from the player and would often, for no clear reason, make negative comments about him to the media. In the many interviews he had given after the Asian Games defeat, Nayeem claimed that Baichung had used a rubber sole on the slushy ground against Japan and had thus underperformed. As many as sixteen years later, he still claims Baichung was responsible for the defeat.

A few players who had been part of the Asian Games team felt that India could have at least drawn the game had Baichung bought a new pair of hard soles. Baichung had repeatedly skidded on the slushy pitch and had clearly not been in his element that day, which may have upset the former coach. There is truth in the saying, 'Where there is smoke, there is fire', but the ego tussle between Nayeem and Baichung went out of control as the coach's prejudice slowly turned into a more personal grudge against the player over the years.

I don't underestimate Nayeem's greatness as a coach. He was the first Indian coach to cross swords with the clubs and the AIFF in order to provide better facilities to players—right from arranging for mineral water, a proper diet and five-star accommodation. He enjoys a great deal of respect for his knowledge of the game but where he fell short in his heyday was in managing players the way P.K. Banerjee or Amal Dutta could. P.K., in his capacity as the coach of the national team, or during his years with Mohun Bagan and East Bengal in the 1970s and 80s, had cleverly managed a host of star players. He never involved himself in their personal problems, but sorted out issues like a friend and philosopher. He always had a great sense of humour which brought him closer to his players. Dutta, too, knew instinctively how to handle stars and never got into ego wars with them. With P.K. and Dutta, respect, as far as the players were concerned, was mutual and this earned these legendary coaches a place in their hearts. In sharp contrast, Nayeem's brooding, introverted and soft-spoken nature created a barrier between him and the players. They never tried to interact with him on a personal level. Some of his contemporaries, both in Hyderabad and in Calcutta, felt that Nayeem was too rigid in his coaching and his interaction with the players.

With Baichung, Nayeem could have shown a bigger heart and doused the flames instead of allowing it to spread to the media, the clubs and the very players who were reluctant to join the club that he coached.

In his comments, Nayeem would always praise I.M. Vijayan over Baichung and draw the two into unnecessary comparisons. Vijayan came from a very poor family and didn't have any formal schooling, but he was extremely talented and often was highly rated by all his coaches, including Nayeem.

However, Baichung's good looks, besides his skill, made him the darling of the media and he soon became the face of Indian football. TV cameras followed him wherever he played in the country and he was always in the news. All these were reason enough to alienate Nayeem, who was also biased against Baichung's North-eastern teammates because of their style of dressing and hairdos.

As a coach, Nayeem was entrusted with the responsibility of infusing team spirit in his players. Instead he continually drew parallels between two players of two vastly different cultures and states, disregarding the inherent differences in their outlook and way of life. By hailing Vijayan as a disciplined player, Nayeem conveyed that Baichung was not. Nayeem should have judged Baichung by the yardstick of his performance and not by what he did off the field and whom he talked to, but the coach got far too involved in his personal life.

Nayeem would try to negate all of Baichung's achievements and once even said that Vijayan was technically superior to him. As most football experts would agree, both these players had different styles: Vijayan had a silken touch, and Baichung had an amazing burst of speed and a killer instinct which was an unbeatable combination inside the penalty box. It was an entirely unnecessary comparison as the two players formed a formidable pair both in the Indian team and in JCT.

The Nayeem versus Baichung saga remained a hot topic for the media. Many a time, the media drew comparisons with the Sourav Ganguly–Greg Chappel controversy in Indian cricket in 2005, which ultimately saw the exit of Chappel.

Unlike Sourav, Baichung, however, never retaliated against Nayeem. He has always been particular about keeping himself away from controversies, only intent on playing his game and focussing on his training. He always shrugged off his coach's criticism as just 'one of those things' and, whenever asked for his reactions by the media, maintained that 'harmony' had been restored.

Nayeem's pointed criticism, which many feel is baseless, didn't go down too well with the football fraternity. He compromised his own reputation by his discriminatory behaviour. In March 2006, when Nayeem was sacked by AIFF, the frustrated coach went overboard with his criticism of Baichung, particularly after India's 0–3 defeat against Yemen at Delhi's Ambedkar Stadium. This eventually led to his downfall; Nayeem coached India for the last time in March 2006.

Baichung, in true professional spirit, has only played down the controversy. He commented, though, that he would have quit football in 2006 had it not been for the national coach who had succeeded Nayeemuddin, Bob Houghton. He had seriously been contemplating retirement after his falling out with Nayeemuddin, but changed his mind after speaking to Houghton and the then AIFF president, Priya Ranjan Dasmunshi. Baichung then went on to lead India to the Nehru Cup title in 2007 and 2009, followed by another triumph in the AFC Challenge in 2008, which earned India a berth in the 2011 Asian Cup for the first time since 1984. 'I was not enjoying my football [in 2006] because of the prevailing situation at that time. I then spoke to Bob, who was taking over as coach. Dasmunshi, too, didn't want me to retire. Changes in the management encouraged me to change my mind about retirement,' said Baichung.

Why a traitor?

When he announced his retirement in December 2011, Nayeem sparked off a controversy once again. The coach who had been sacked unceremoniously in March 2006 after India's defeats against Japan and Yemen in the Asian Cup qualifiers, blamed the former India captain for the country's poor performance and demanded a CBI inquiry into the matches five and a half years later. Nayeem branded Baichung a traitor and even accused him of plotting against the coach—with the support of his teammates—before the match against Yemen. 'He conspired with the players and didn't allow the goalkeeping coach (Atanu Bhattacharya) to be present at the team meeting. He got it done with only six to seven players of the team present,' Nayeem alleged. He claimed that Baichung, celebrated as India's football icon, had betrayed the country.

Nayeem's accusations were mostly laughed at and not given any importance. Surprisingly though, a day after accusing Baichung of match-rigging, the former coach apologized.

After several interviews with Nayeem, I am no nearer to fathoming his intense dislike of Baichung. Whenever I have asked him about his animosity towards Baichung and his reasons for the same, the ex-coach has struggled to give me a convincing reply. 'It was a misunderstanding. I had no personal enmity with him. I had committed a mistake,' he managed to tell me once in 2011.

However, and most interestingly, I discovered that Nayeem was not the only coach to dislike Baichung.

During one of my visits to the Air Force Bal Bharti School trials in Delhi in 2009, Syed Shahid Hakim, India's respected FIFA referee and former India coach, pointed to one of his co-spotters and former India international Ranjit Thapa. 'See, I would rate him as the best striker. He is much more talented than what you football writers think about Baichung, who's just an ordinary player,' he told me. Hakim, like Nayeem, is known for his outspoken and often brash approach. More erudite than most former Indian footballers, Hakim has held top positions in the administration of the Indian Air Force and SAI besides having donned Indian colours at the Rome Olympics.

Close on the heels of Baichung's retirement news, two other former coaches, Shabbir Ali and Subrata Bhattacharya, also mocked his achievements, thus joining the bandwagon of Baichung-bashers. 'I'm not saying he wasn't a good player, but calling him the face of Indian football is nothing but a media creation,' Shabbir, Indian football's star striker in the 1980s, who later turned coach for several clubs and was a technical director in the national team in 1995, told the media after Baichung's retirement. Shabbir believed that Baichung had got 'too much with minimum effort'.

'He played against the third division teams in Dubai and Portugal and India lost. Everybody knows what happened during the Asian Cup in Doha where he played with an injury and occupied a place in the side, with the AIFF becoming a laughing stock,' said Shabbir.

Bhattacharya, who has played for and coached the Bagan and East Bengal teams, called Baichung 'India's David Beckham' and went on to suggest that Baichung had good PR skills and knew how to present himself to the media. He even dismissed Baichung, calling him a 'bad footballer' who only scored goals against weaker teams like Nepal, Bangladesh, Bhutan, and Maldives.

Moving away from such criticism and rivalries, I remember what the German national captain Philip Lahm said about Baichung at his farewell match in Delhi. 'The only thing that I know about Indian football is Baichung,' said the Bayern Munich star.

Among the few Indian coaches who admired the potential in Baichung was P.K., a living legend of Indian football. The former Indian captain was Baichung's coach when the latter evolved into India's number one striker and became famous for his hat-trick against Bagan in a match that saw a record attendance at Salt Lake Stadium in Calcutta. P.K. knew how to handle talented players like Baichung, more so because he was experienced in managing the best of Indian and club teams, including Bagan and East Bengal.

During one of my interviews with the legend at his Salt Lake residence, he spoke appreciatively of Baichung. 'Baichung reminded me of Neville D'Souza and Mewalal. He was so quick inside the box, just like them,' said the septuagenarian.

It is interesting to see how the same footballer can generate such polarized opinions from the sport's veterans. Most great athletes do think they are the best. But Baichung hadn't announced to the world, like Muhammad Ali had, that he was the greatest footballer. He is still just as grounded and dignified as he was when he started out. Often criticized for locking horns with Indian coaches, Baichung clarifies that he has no axe to grind against them. 'I have no problem with Indian coaches. I just wanted the best and the most knowledgeable man for the job. We have to accept that Indian football is nowhere, even on the Asian stage. The players need to learn a lot to bridge that gap. The same applies to our coaches too. I have benefited from all the foreign coaches. (Rustam) Akhramov changed my life by promoting me from a midfielder to a striker. But we had the best success under Bob.'

He credits the South Africa-based Englishman for the turnaround in his career. According to him, Bob Houghton was a favourite among the players because the Englishman never bothered about their off-the-field activities. Under Houghton and Stephen Constantine, who also served as national coach from 2001–04, Baichung flourished. By and large, he favoured the foreign coaches for their broad thinking and professionalism. This could be another reason why he was so hated by the Indian coaches. The three years that Baichung spent with Bury FC in England also contributed to his understanding and appreciation of how relevant modern football coaching was to a player.

Liberalism era

Baichung forged a great understanding with Houghton, probably India's most successful coach in recent times. In Doha, before India's second group match against Bahrain in the Asian Cup held in January 2011, Houghton said that Baichung's influence on Indian national football is much like Sachin Tendulkar's on Indian cricket.

'The best cricketer in the world is in India. Tendulkar is a very fine role model, a fine person. Comparison with Baichung is inevitable. They are of the same age, they keep going. He is a major influence on the team both on and off the field. He is a leader,' Houghton told the international media in the Qatari capital.

Their understanding was one of the main reasons behind India's fabulous run and victory in three international tournaments. While other Indian coaches have held back no criticism for Baichung, Houghton's support for him gave rise to a popular belief that the Englishman actually fell back on Baichung to extend his coaching stint with the national team. His success with the national team was limited to two Nehru Cup wins in 2007 and 2009 and the AFC Challenge Cup in 2008 and most of our former coaches observe that all these triumphs had taken place at home. Houghton didn't have any achievements abroad and Nayeem often said that with the huge budgets allocated for the Indian teams and a five-figure salary to the Englishman, Indian coaches could have done much better had they been given the same facilities.

Both Houghton and Baichung had great respect for each other and even the media started observing that the coach invariably chipped in to support the injury-prone Baichung between 2009 and 2011.

'Indian football has had a role model who has been positive. He was someone all young and aspiring footballers could look up to. Having worked with him for the last five years, I've been constantly aware of the great respect that players had for him—not only in India, but also around the continent and even beyond, after his appearances in World XIs numerous times,' said Houghton when Baichung announced his retirement in September 2011.

I am reminded of an incident which may shed some light on the widely varying approaches of the Nayeem and Houghton eras.

In 2005, when the Indian players stepped out of the bus at Thyagaraj Stadium in south Delhi, where the national team under Nayeem was preparing for the SAFF Cup in Islamabad, a sort of strict silence gripped them. The players quietly lined up at the side and waited for the coach's instructions. Baichung, Renedy, and the others looked grim and the stadium seemed to have turned into a camp for strict regimental training, where a smile would have been met with punishment. No one talked. Even the journalists who covered the camp felt that Nayeem's training lacked spirit and joie-de-vivre.

One of the members of the 1998 Asian Games said on condition of anonymity that Nayeem was a great coach, but his method of handling the players was 'out of this world'.

The player went on to narrate an incident that demonstrated Nayeem's straitjacket approach. 'We were all set to clear immigration at Calcutta airport, but as soon as Nayeem saw journalists and photographers there, he instructed us to wear the team blazers and do some stretching!' he said.

'To wear a tie and put on a blazer in that stuffy weather was something nobody liked, but we couldn't utter a single word.

'Even in the Bangkok hotel, he used to keep his door ajar throughout the evening to keep an eye on our movements. We used to avoid him because if he found anyone crossing his room he would immediately call us in and engage us in long-drawn meetings even in the late hours. We still respect his coaching philosophies, but some of his methods were boring and outdated,' said the player.

Things changed dramatically when Houghton took over as coach in June 2006. The body language of the players said all that one needed to know about his liberalism era.

The Englishman, a former Fulham player, was revered for his credentials: he had earlier coached Sweden's Malmo FC in 1974. He gained fame after his team reached the 1979 European Cup final, losing 1–0 against Nottingham Forest.

It was the first and only time a Swedish team had reached the European Cup final. The national federation provided Houghton with better facilities than the Indian coaches, but he made the centrally located Ambedkar Stadium his preferred training centre.

The Englishman ensured that the players gave their best on the field, and yet believed in giving them their freedom, and consequently, the footballers enjoyed training under him.

'He never interfered,' said Baichung, who played under several coaches in his long international career. 'All he wanted was that we give a 100 per cent to our training and to the matches. There was no favouritism. That's why he was respected so much by all of us.'

While Nayeem distanced himself from his best player, Houghton comforted Baichung whenever he was in trouble, which strengthened their bond. The understanding between the manager and the captain was reflected in the team's performances: under Houghton, India played fast, attacking, and successful football. Nayeem's team didn't perform simply because there was no love lost between him and the players. His 'conspiracy' theory about Baichung was not proved and Nayeem quickly did a U-turn a day after calling him traitor.

Without naming Nayeem, Baichung has often said that Indian coaches should change their 1960s' mindset and bring themselves up to speed with modern football. Barcelona's stupendous success is a case in point—the technical finesse incorporated into the team by the workaholic Pep Guardiola and the excellent relationship he shared with his star players, Lionel Messi, Iniesta, Xavi and others, led the club to some of its greatest triumphs, winning the Champions League, La Liga and FIFA Club World Cup.

Modern coaching entails an understanding of the players' psyches, instead of simply shouting out instructions at training sessions. A player, whether he is a star or a rookie, needs support and encouragement from his manager. However, if a player finds that he is being subjected to mental humiliation, he will naturally lose interest in the game. This could well be the reason why Baichung decided to quit in 2006.

While Baichung and his team excelled under Houghton's guidance, some of our own coaches continued to criticize the national team. They claimed that both Houghton and Baichung 'used each other' for mutual survival. The Indian coaches accused Houghton of earning too much and suggested that the former India skipper had achieved nothing in the recent past. However, they quite conveniently forgot to mention the duo's contribution to the Indian team, which won its maiden Nehru Cup title in 2007. Two years later, India repeated the feat at Houghton's favourite Ambedkar Stadium.

Indian football gained a lot of visibility and importance in the national media thanks to Houghton and Baichung. For the first time, the Indian football team looked glamorous, with spotlights trained on its two most important members.

Unlike his Indian predecessors, Houghton never criticized his players. When India was battered 4–0 by the Socceroos in the Asian Cup at Doha's Al Sadd Stadium and again by Bahrain (5–2) and by South Korea (4–1), Houghton never lost his cool. In sharp contrast to Nayeem's outburst against Baichung in Bangkok in 1998, Houghton didn't blame his players for the failure. Instead, he cleverly placed the blame on the faulty football system in the country. While it may have seemed as though he was seeking refuge in excuses, Houghton asserted that given the limited facilities available to his team, they had achieved the best they could by qualifying for the prestigious Asian tournament.

In the pre-and post-match press conferences, he would dwell on players like Baichung, Renedy, and Gouramangi and the difficulties they faced when they had started playing professional football in India. In return, Baichung was vocal about his support for the Englishman, whether with regard to his selections or his bitter fights with the national federation. Such bonding helped the Indian team during Houghton's stint. In another impressive instance, in 2010, when Houghton got embroiled in a racism controversy with referee Dinesh Nair, the entire team, including Baichung, backed their coach unconditionally. 'I've played under him for the last five years and can assure you that Bob is not a racist. I think Dinesh had crossed the line and took it too far,' said Baichung.

Houghton, too, never left Baichung's side when the skipper was engaged in a battle with Mohun Bagan in 2009. Houghton said, 'I was astonished to see the commitment and dedication of our Indian team captain questioned. I have coached international players of more than thirty countries and have never found a more committed and dedicated player.'

When Houghton resigned in April 2011, there was a major uproar. Both the media and the football fraternity were shocked by his sudden decision. Sources say that the Englishman was forced to quit so that the charges of racism against him could be dropped. 'I don't know if it is a battle of egos or purely because of non-performance, which the AIFF insists it is. One thing that I know is that this is a very, very sad day for Indian football. If the AIFF thinks that Houghton hasn't done a good job then I don't know how their thinking goes,' Baichung was quoted as saying to *DNA*. 'I think the thing that went against the coach was the poor performances and the comments he made in Doha regarding the infrastructure. But even former AFC president Mohammed bin Hammam has criticized India's poor infrastructure,' he explained.

Besides Baichung, almost all the senior players, including Sunil Chhetri, Renedy Singh, Mahesh Gawli, N.P. Pradeep and Dipak Mondol, expressed their disappointment over the way the AIFF handled the Houghton issue. So much so that the federation had to issue a 'show-cause' to the players for their attempts to take on the national body. What angered the players most was the unceremonious manner in which India's most successful coach had to leave the game.

'I had all but retired from football in 2006. But he coaxed me out of it and made me believe in my abilities,' said Baichung.

'I owe him big time for that. It was a dream for the players of my generation to play in the Asian Cup. For a player from our continent, that's the biggest tournament after the World Cup,' he added.

Not surprisingly, then, after Houghton's exit in April, Baichung, too, followed suit. He announced his retirement just four months later.

5

Import to the Motherland of Football

In his early years when Arsene Wenger joined Arsenal as their manager, the Frenchman said that he wanted only those players in his team who showed complete commitment and dedication in everything they did and said.

In the context of Indian football, Baichung was known for such commitment and dedication. These rare qualities were what enabled him to make the unlikely journey from East Bengal to Bury in 1999 on a three-year contract.

Though football has been played in India ever since the British introduced it over a century ago, Baichung was only the second Indian—after Mohammad Salim who played for the Celtics in the 1930s—to play professional football outside his homeland.

It was in 1998 that he first considered a move to the West, knowing that it would give him the right kind of exposure. During those years, player management was an unknown concept in most Indian clubs. Former players or NRIs were the ones who acted as agents. Raj Purohit, an NRI, took Baichung under his wing.

'Raj had business interests in England. He was looking for an Indian player and got in touch with a few people in India, including Chuni Goswami, who recommended my name to him. That's how we met,' said Baichung.

When Neil Warnock signed Baichung Bhutia in 1999 for Bury, Indian football writers got a shot in the arm. Baichung's move to England coincided with the NFL's downslide in popularity. After two great seasons following its kick-off in 1996, it was slowly losing its charm. At a time like this, Baichung's import to the motherland of football gave the Indian media, both national and regional, quite a lot to write about.

Baichung did whatever it took to break barriers and make the hitherto uncharted journey to Europe. This is why he remains the only face associated with Indian football even today. Years later, his Bury stint found a place in Gitarattan Jindal Public School's assessment test chapter titled 'Bengal to Bury'.

In May 2000, I travelled to the Netaji Subhas National Institute of Sports (NSNIS) headquarters in Patiala to cover the Indian team's first-ever England tour. On a rather humid and stuffy night, there was a major power failure on campus, including the players' dormitory. It was pitch dark, not to mention uncomfortably hot. After dinner I decided to take a stroll around the sprawling green NSNIS campus. It was during my walk that I chanced upon I.M. Vijayan, Jo Paul Ancheri, and a couple of others roaming around the campus bare-chested and in their shorts. Unable to sleep in the hot and stuffy rooms of the NSNIS, they had decided to get some fresh air. They were laughing and joking, but not once did they complain about the power cut or the uncomfortable rooms in which they had been accommodated.

News of the shoddy facilities provided to star players like Vijayan and Ancheri, and the national team as a whole, at the Patiala camp wasn't reported in the media. But it would hardly have created any ripples. In India, the condition and treatment of players in any sport except cricket is pathetic and nobody dares to protest against the system. Both Vijayan and Ancheri were much bigger stars than Baichung at the time. Like Baichung, they too were mild-natured and simply adjusted to the unprofessional set-up in Indian football. On that hot festering night, when these superstars were wiping their sweat-drenched bodies with their T-shirts, Baichung was far away in the cool climes of Greater Manchester, training in a professional club.

Baichung had gone through similar struggles, but he had always been clear about his goals. Instead of pointlessly raising his voice against the system, he decided to look for newer pastures.

'Vijayan and Ancheri had the potential and talent to play abroad. But they probably didn't try or get any agent. Baichung was motivated to do the right thing at the right time. After he did well in the inaugural NFL in 1996, he was on the lookout for an agent who could take him abroad,' said former India and Air India captain Godfred Pereira.

Bhaskar and players of his time weren't too keen to even try their luck in foreign leagues. Homesickness was one of the main factors that held him back. During Bhaskar's era, in the mid-1970s and 80s, several others got offers from the cash-rich Middle East nations, but all of them preferred to stay put rather than take the opportunity which came their way. 'In the 1970s, I once got an offer from a Kuwaiti club. They were impressed by me and Surajit Sengupta when we toured the country with the national team. But we thought it would be better to play in Calcutta than to earn extra money outside. I guess most Indian footballers are wary about their future, particularly when it comes to playing in a foreign country,' said Bhaskar, a former Indian captain and goalkeeper.

Baichung, however, wanted to be different from his ilk. He didn't once hesitate to take the plunge even if it resulted in failure. He wanted to experiment and in the end was partially successful in fulfilling his dream.

Godfred, now Air India's chief coach, saw Baichung evolve into a mature player, having come a long way from the shy Sikkimese under-16 player of 1992. 'After he came back from England, Baichung was a more well-rounded player. There was a visible difference from when he started in 1992. His confidence and approach to the game were impressive and that's all because of his stint in Bury FC,' reasoned Godfred.

In a developing country whose population touched the one-billion mark in 1998, the costs of setting up a workable domestic game proved a near-insurmountable barrier, particularly when cricket has always reigned as the national obsession. But when the FIFA 1986 World Cup was televised live in India, there was a surge of interest. A decade later, India's corporate sector took a keen interest, which paved the way for the inception of NFL in 1996. But in just three years, the tournament's popularity dipped; interest among the clubs and players waned, spiking only during a derby between East Bengal and Mohun Bagan.

Baichung was sharper than the rest, both in skill and intelligence. As a youngster who came from the hills, he remained grounded and disciplined, and wasn't easily swayed by the kind of demigod status he earned while playing for East Bengal in Calcutta. A bachelor at the time, he stayed at his modest flat in Kankurgachi and then in Salt Lake on the eastern fringes of the city.

Baichung knew Calcutta was a great place to start his career. But he was never keen on prolonging his stay there. At the back of his mind, he knew he wanted a change and better opportunities. Even at that early stage in his career, he appreciated the marketing side of the game and signed some endorsement deals. When he saw that the NFL was losing its charm, he wanted to experience an environment in which the game generated more excitement and showcased greater quality.

'During one of our discussions, I suggested that it was high time he tried his luck abroad. Though he knew it would be a challenge, he decided to give it a shot. He doesn't care about success or failure, but would never leave a job half done,' said his sister Kunzang.

Before he joined Bury, he had several unsuccessful trials at Aston Villa, Fulham, and West Bromwich Albion. He spent two weeks on trial at Villa, but returned home after he failed to impress John Gregory, who chose to go for top names.

After such an unsuccessful venture, very few would have had the confidence to send their CVs to top clubs in England. But Baichung remained confident and resolute.

Today, he admits that a move to a Premiership club so soon had been a little too ambitious.

'I didn't expect to get into the Aston Villa team so easily. It was a good experience for me to be at their trials. But the climate change from warm to cold didn't help me. I spent five days with the club and enjoyed it,' he said.

Leading Premier League clubs had visited and enjoyed considerable commercial success in China, Japan, South Korea, Thailand and other developing nations. Bury, which has a large South Asian population of mostly Punjabis and Bangladeshis in their town, wanted to attract the Asian market. The then Bury chairman, Terry Robinson, had hoped to cash in on Baichung to attract British Asian fans and inspire local youngsters who mostly stayed away from football for fear of racial abuse.

The powers that be of English football also believed there was an enormous market to tap into in terms of future TV revenue and wanted to bet on a top-class Indian footballer. Kick It Out, an anti-racism organization that ran a catchy campaign called 'Let's Kick Racism out of Football', welcomed Baichung's arrival and believed that it was an effort to inspire Asian players across Britain to follow in his footsteps. They hoped football would eventually take off among Asians in the same way that it did among Afro-Caribbeans in the past.

A difficult journey

On 2 October, 1999, Baichung made history by becoming the first footballer from independent India to play in England when he donned the Bury colours in a Division II League tie. When he arrived at Bury, his boyish looks drew comparisons with Liverpool striker Michael Owen.

His three seasons in England gained a lot of media attention, but his career didn't take off as well as he had hoped, as he spent most of his time on the bench. During a chat with me, Oliver Kay, chief football correspondent of the *Times* in London, made this accurate observation about Baichung's Bury stint: 'Bhutia's arrival at the time had a lot of interest in it, but it seems to have disappeared. I only ever saw him play once, because I didn't cover Bury matches very often and he didn't play very often. I was told he found the change in lifestyle quite difficult. On the one occasion I watched him play, I remember that he struggled to make an impact. He didn't seem physically strong enough to play in English football—in that type of team, at least,' said Kay. 'I think Bury signed him more for commercial reasons than football reasons. I know that they hoped he would succeed on the pitch, but it didn't really seem like they were convinced he would.'

Many things had gone wrong for Baichung. The first mistake was joining Bury mid-season when his fitness level wasn't the same as that of the rest of the squad.

'As I settled down, I had a knee injury and was off for six months. That meant I had a really quiet season. When such a thing happens, your chances of looking for another club in England or Europe obviously diminish,' said Baichung.

Like most of his contemporaries and predecessors in Indian football, Baichung never got the right kind of fitness guidance. Foremost among the problems ailing football in India at the time, was this: Indian clubs lacked multi-gym or fitness facilities and, as a result, the players suffered when they competed against teams from South Korea, Japan, Iran and the Middle East.

'I joined Bury mid-season. They had by that time finished their pre-season training. Warnock knew I needed to make a lot of adjustments when it came to the physical aspects, climate and fitness,' he added. 'This is what we lack in India. We don't want to work systematically and nobody is bothered. At the Gigg Lane, training facilities were excellent. The club looked after each and every player. During the off season, too, players were instructed to follow certain exercises to maintain their fitness,' he said.

Poor fitness was cited as one of the reasons that kept him on the bench. But as everybody in India knows, a player has to go through the grind to reach this level. Playing on Calcutta's slushy grounds, with poor facilities and no fitness training to speak of, has ruined many a career.

Baichung insists, though, that it is unfair to compare Indian and British players. 'The pre-season training is very technical and also very physical. In India, we just run for hours in the heat during training which is quite different in England and elsewhere,' he said.

He made a lot of small adjustments when he reached England six years after making his debut for East Bengal.

'Right from 1993, I was used to playing in the heat. So, initially in England, the cold was a huge problem. The game was very fast and physical,' he added.

Preece wanted to prove a point.

Another problem cropped up when coach Warnock resigned. It was he who had been impressed with Baichung during the trials and signed him on. 'Baichung was a superb signing for us. He is very sharp in the 18-yard box,' said Warnock, who left Bury to join Sheffield United in December 1999.

After Warnock left, senior teammates Steve Redmond and Andy Preece became joint caretaker–managers in Bury. Preece was appointed manager on a permanent basis at the end of the season, while Redmond became player–assistant manager.

'When Warnock left the club, it was the biggest disaster for me. I had to struggle for the work permit and that meant a considerable amount of time was lost. It became difficult to catch up for the pre-season. But when I really caught up and slowly began to get better, he left,' Baichung rued.

When Preece took over, Baichung didn't fit into his game plan. Bury played the old British style, which was more of long ball in the air and a lot of physical effort. The team's requirement was a tall and strong striker. Though he was used as a striker, the former Indian captain warmed the bench more often and it got increasingly frustrating.

'Anyone would get frustrated if they didn't get to do the things they love most,' he said. 'Warnock understood that I could fit into his game plan. I was given extra training to make me adjust to the system quickly. Unfortunately, he quit and I was left a bit disappointed. It's important for a player to have a coach who can trust him,' explained Baichung.

'Preece was a striker himself. So he wanted to prove to the club management that the coaching reins were in safe hands as he doubled as a player and a coach. When I was getting better in terms of performance and confidence, I was sidelined.'

His journey was fraught with more difficulties—his work permit was originally turned down but he won his appeal and made his debut for the Shakers on 3 October, 1999, in the 3–2 win against Cardiff City.

In that match, he came on as a substitute for Ian Lawson and played a part in Bury's second goal, which was scored by Darren Bullock after Baichung's volley was deflected into his path.

He played in front of a few thousand people at Gigg Lane in his debut match, in stark contrast to the matches he had played for East Bengal in Calcutta.

Homesick and lonely

Baichung stayed in an apartment and learnt to cook, though it was mostly fast and instant fare like pasta, mashed potatoes, and lots of meat. As a 23-year-old, he quickly adapted to life in England and became self-reliant.

More than the physical hardship, overcoming his frame of mind must have been the real challenge during his stay in England.

'It was a lonely life out there with hardly any friends around. I only knew one Robin Singh who used to stay close to our apartment. There were limited opportunities to go out,' he added. 'I used to get up at 8.30 a.m., have my breakfast and leave for the training sessions. It was a 5-minute walk from the apartment. We used to finish by 1 p.m. I would then return for lunch.'

His routine soon turned monotonous and homesickness set in during the second season.

'Homesickness was a big reason for choosing to come back. The weather was bad and I wasn't getting a chance to play. All these factors forced me to accept that it was better to return to India,' he added.

Madhuri, who married Baichung in 2004, said that he used to stay in touch with her through emails during those years.

'He used to mail me about his loneliness there. He even wrote to my father, asking if he would allow me to visit England,' said Madhuri.

Despite feeling out of place in England, Baichung sparkled in matches whenever he got a chance to play for Bury.

On 15 April 2000, he scored his first goal in the league against Chesterfield, but a recurring knee injury limited him to only three games in his final season with Bury. His final appearance, on 27 August 2001, saw a 3–0 defeat to Swindon Town. He aggravated his injury, attempting a comeback in November, and had to undergo another operation. In all, he made forty-six appearances for the Lancashire club, including twenty as a substitute, and scored three goals.

'In the pre-season of the third year at Bury, I did well before I got injured,' he said.

He was finally released after the cash-strapped club was placed in administration. 'It wasn't Baichung's fault that he couldn't cut it in England. He was an outsider, and it's tough enough for those born and raised in England or anywhere in Europe to break the glass ceiling,' explained Kay.

Baichung acknowledged that he tasted only moderate success in England and that it was an eye-opener for someone who came from a country where facilities are limited and a professional approach is sadly lacking.

'I always wanted to learn. Playing for the national team and the clubs in India helped me a lot. But I wanted to learn about international football. My stint in England taught me so much. Right from club management and the role of managers, everything I witnessed there changed my notion about international football,' he said.

Baichung got to play alongside his childhood heroes like David Beckham and Andy Cole. His one regret is that he couldn't score against Manchester United in a friendly match.

'It's definitely one of my best moments as a player. Man United had only international players. That was my best match in England. I should have scored a goal, but hit the crossbar. The only goal I scored was ruled as an offside,' said Baichung.

'My Bury experience has been a combination of good and bad,' he reminisced.

Bury experience inspired Chhetris and Pauls

Yet he showed his Indian teammates that playing in England was not impossible. A decade later, his juniors in the national team—Sunil Chhetri, Gouramangi Singh and Subrata Paul—tried their luck in trials abroad. One cannot ignore Baichung's role in changing the mindset of the next generation of players.

Chhetri signed for Kansas City Wizards in Major League Soccer in 2010, thus becoming the third player of note from the subcontinent to go abroad. After a modest stint there, he returned home and once again left India to sign for Sporting Clube de Portugal of the Primeira Liga where he would play for the club's reserve side.

In 2010, Gouramangi was called upon by Melbourne Heart for a trial in the A-League, which, despite his reportedly impressing Heart staff, was unsuccessful. It was mutually decided that the Indian defender would not get the opportunity in the first team which already had star players.

'Going to Australia was a great experience. Although nothing came out of it, I got to witness the professionalism and standard of a much higher league. Bhai (Baichung) recommended that I should go there and just give my best as he had done in England,' said Gouramangi. 'Bhai has inspired not just me, but many others. I played under his captaincy for many years and have always tried to pick up whatever I could from him,' added the Manipuri defender.

Paul, the first Indian goalkeeper to join a top-division side in Europe, was offered a contract from 1 January to 30 June, 2014 by FC Vikings, also known as FC Vestsjælland, after a three-week trial stint with the club last year.

Agreed, Baichung didn't play in the Olympics. In truth, as the standard of Asian teams got better and better, Indian teams just couldn't match up and never really made much of an impact in the tough Olympic qualifiers. India has not qualified for the Summer Games after the 1960 Rome Olympics. Yet, Baichung stood tall among contemporary Indian sportspersons because of his tenacity to survive against the odds. And that may be the reason why every youngster in the North-east tries to identify himself with him even today.

'I've spent a month in Manipur with the best under-20 kids. They all knew Messi, Ronaldo, Rooney and Baichung, and a few knew Chhetri. None could name the other Indian players or the I-League teams,' said Steve Darby who had coached Bagan for a few months in 2011.

Turning semi-professional at the age of sixteen, Baichung became one of India's highest paid players. He preferred to devote himself to the game and never took up any other job. It would have been easy for him to settle down in his comfort zone in Calcutta, but he moved ahead with a pragmatic approach and a level head on his shoulders. In a country where a career in sports is considered risky and unsustainable, Baichung proves otherwise.

Looking back, Baichung stands by each of his decisions, particularly his stint in England. 'It was an eye-opener for me to gain first-hand experience of the professionalism in England. English clubs are successful because they know how to run the game,' said Baichung, who also had spells in Malaysia, having played for Perak FC in 2003 and Selangor in 2005.

Come to think of it, he has been able to put his Bury experience to use in his own club, United Sikkim.

'All these English clubs have youth development projects with good training facilities and coaching. When I created my own club, my first priority was to have a full-fledged youth base. The idea of launching football schools was the first big step. Besides, we also conduct various training programmes in Sikkim where our coaches hold weekly sessions with the kids,' he said.

As former *Times* journalist Peter Lansley, who in 2000

covered the Indian football team's first England tour since 1948, said, 'Building bridges across the continents by trading of talent and experience may be the first step to establishing Indian football once and for all at home and in foreign fields.'

Baichung's Bury stint has had a huge impact on Indian football. With the import of India's best footballing star to England, there has been a growing interest among top English Premier League clubs that have realized the potential of an Indian market where their brands can be sold through merchandise and by sending their grass-roots level coaches to big cities like Delhi and Mumbai. The clubs have tied up with various schools to draw the kids in week-long coaching camps, while annual promotional events scout the best talents who are then offered a month-long training in the respective clubs. Academies have sprouted in almost all the schools and inter-school events for all age groups are now seen as the way forward. The single most important advantage of this has been that the national federation which had been snoozing all these years, has woken up to the benefits of having a full-time academy programme to develop the sport at the grass-roots.

Nowadays, most European clubs—from Manchester United to Chelsea, Arsenal, Liverpool and Barcelona—target young Indian footballers, offering them the chance to stay and train at their youth camps for anything between a fortnight and a month. Obviously, there is a marketing side to this, but such initiatives have done a world of good to young players.

Baichung was not a product of any academy as the concept did not exist in his home state. During and before his time, it was the local coaches or scouts who used to play a major role in nurturing talent. Today, that age-old system has been upgraded and Baichung can take the entire credit for infusing the concepts he picked up during his years with Bury. His own chain of football schools under the banner of Baichung Bhutia Football School (BBFS) is one bright example of incorporating western knowhow to great effect. Students at his schools get the best of rudimentary lessons from qualified foreign coaches. Baichung is firm on one thing: the kids must be given the best possible facilities and training from a very young age. No wonder BBFS initially hired coaches from Football by Carlos Queiroz, the renowned soccer school started by the former Portuguese and Real Madrid coach, who also assisted Sir Alex Ferguson at Manchester United.

Today, with most English and Spanish clubs marketing their brands in Indian cities, Baichung can take some of the credit for having introduced the Indian market to these foreign clubs. Before 1999, foreign clubs didn't feel the need to invest in Indian clubs or schools, even though they promoted their brands targeting India's substantial pool of urban youth. But once Baichung hit the headlines in England, it was a sort of awakening for these European clubs.

6

Dancing Shoes

When the Rishi Kapoor-starrer *Karz* was released in 1980, a 4-year-old Baichung hung on to the actor's every move. Although he would later become an ardent fan of Aamir Khan, young Baichung was at the time fascinated by both Rishi Kapoor and Mithun Chakraborty. While Rishi's musical blockbusters made an impression on him, Mithun's dance moves in *Disco Dancer* floored him.

In 2009, Baichung replaced his football studs with dancing shoes to take part in the third season of the dance reality show *Jhalak Dikhhla Jaa*. He enthralled the audience and the judges to walk away with the title, beating the nimble-footed actress Gauhar Khan and crowd favourite, TV actor Karan Singh Grover. He became the first Indian sportsperson to win the show, crafted in the format of BBC One's *Strictly Come Dancing*, where celebrities put on their dancing shoes and compete, aided by their choreographer–dancer partners.

Baichung got the audience on his side with an energetic performance of his childhood favourite, 'I am a disco dancer', his skills sharpened by his partner Sonia Jaffer. Later, he put on a splendid show as a finalist with Sonia on a track from *Don* interspersed with Shahrukh Khan's famous dialogues, followed by 'Chance pe dance' from *Rab Ne Bana Di Jodi*. 'I'm not a great dancer, but I've grown up watching both Rishi Kapoor and Mithunda dance in Hindi movies. I've admired them a lot. Mithunda's *Disco Dancer* has been one of my favourite films. I guess I only wanted to experience something like that,' said Baichung.

The show, which started on 27 February, 2009 and ended on 31 May the same year, was Baichung's chance to earn big money and generate great publicity for himself, all in a short span of time. He was also keen to get involved in something that had nothing to do with football and would give him that extra mileage. But his critics believed that the former Indian captain was willing to do anything to reclaim the limelight since his career was coming to a gradual but inevitable end, and his form had nosedived as well. These claims, however, don't hold weight as Baichung had some memorable tournaments in 2009: winning the Nehru Cup at Delhi's Ambedkar Stadium and completing his 100th match for India, among others.

'You know who introduced me to this show?' he asked me. 'Leander Paes,' he answered before I could hazard a guess. 'Paes didn't like the proposal offered to him and recommended my name to the organizers.'

Though Baichung may seem quiet and reticent, an introvert

even, in the company of close friends and teammates, he knows how to have fun. Often, he can be seen shaking a leg at nightclubs with friends or bantering playfully with teammates. 'I'm a reserved person. If you ask me to get down on the streets and dance, I won't do it. I dance in nightclubs, but that's just about moving wildly. It's not about matching steps to a tune and emoting to convey what the lyrics of the song mean. So, to that extent, it was a challenge that I accepted to be a part of *Jhalak Dikhhla Jaa*,' he said.

For someone like him, shy and without any formal training in dance, it was a huge step to overcome his inhibitions and agree to dance before millions. For the viewers, on the other hand, it was refreshing to watch the impressive footballer, whom they had only seen kicking and whizzing past the best of defenders on the football field, dance to 'Left leg aage aage'.

'When I danced to the title song of *Goal,* the performance was so bad that I wanted to run away. It was only after I crossed the semis that I thought of winning.'

Sonia polishes his dancing skills

Baichung's rise to fame as a dancer can be credited to Sonia Jaffer, a Panjim-based choreographer who was his dance partner and trained the sportsperson in the finer nuances of the art. If Baichung charmed viewers on stage, it was the result of the strenuous rehearsals and practice schedules Sonia put him through. She was determined to make the best use of Baichung's athleticism, and it paid off. In one episode, when the duo was within striking distance of the title, she and

Baichung executed a complex heart-stopping routine on two tables that had been set apart.

Sonia was born to a Tanzanian father and an Indian mother in Mumbai and grew up in Kuwait. She completed her basics in ballet from the Royal School of Dance in London. There was no doubt that she was a competent choreographer—a fact she only reaffirmed by winning the *Jhalak* crown. Sonia, however, hadn't been paired with the footballer initially. 'Except me, every other choreographer had their respective celebs picked out. But my celeb kept changing right from day one. I was getting really frustrated because those initial weeks of rehearsal were crucial in setting the tempo. Three days before the shoot, I still didn't have a celeb assigned to me. I got a call from one of the creative heads asking me how I would feel about moving to Calcutta for the show. By then I couldn't care less. I agreed. I was then told that the next day I would meet my celeb,' said Sonia, who runs the Beaumont Dance Company in Panjim.

'I was in the Passion Room (there are four rehearsal halls in Jhalak House) when Baichung walked in. I was in shock. They had got our football captain!' It only helped that Sonia is a football lover who used to freelance as a journalist for a Goan newspaper. 'To see him in front of me was a surprise and a delight,' she said. 'I knew I had a winner on my hands. As he walked in, to me it seemed as though the Jhalak trophy was walking towards me!' added Sonia with a laugh.

If Rishi Kapoor inspired the Tinkitam icon to shake a leg, Sonia instilled in him the aspiration to become a dancer.

'All we did was rehearse. We did not even have the time to become friends! All our time went in teaching and learning,' she said. 'The *Jhalak* format was such that before we shot for the first episode, we had a period of four to six weeks of rehearsals. He used to yawn in the afternoons and I used to go insane. But you can't blame him because he used to come straight from football trainings to dance rehearsals.'

Baichung knew his limitations as a dancer and was prepared to push himself as far as he could go.

'The theme was given to us by the channel, Sony, which produced the show. I used to select a song and a style of dance that fit. Once that was approved, I briefed the costume designer. I visualized the choreography in my head and then I used to break it down for Baichung,' said Sonia. However, in one instance, Baichung refused to follow Sonia's instructions. 'It was during a tapori dance round. I asked him to be a girl and he simply said no,' laughed Sonia. 'I never tried to cover for him. I gave him simple but authentic steps. If it was salsa, I made sure he did at least the basic steps.'

Trouble beckons

While Baichung was enjoying his stint as a dancer and entertainer, his participation in *Jhalak* inadvertently dragged him into an acrimonious battle with his club and employer, Mohun Bagan. The club slapped Baichung first with a show-cause notice and then followed it up with a suspension for six months on charges of abandoning club duties for dance rehearsals. Baichung had never expected the club to take such action against him.

Initially, as Baichung claimed, Bagan had been okay with him attending rehearsals and had agreed to let him go for the show on the agreement that he wouldn't miss training sessions or matches and would remain committed to the club. It is possible that Bagan officials thought, or hoped, that he would have neither the skill nor the audience support to continue participating in the show.

During his entire career, he had never been admonished or reprimanded by any coach or club, but that changed after Bagan officials began to show their displeasure.

After the I-League ended in April 2009, Bagan lay low. But when Baichung skipped an exhibition match in Jalpaiguri, it didn't go down well with the club. Anjan Mitra, Bagan's general secretary claimed that Baichung had refused to participate in the exhibition match. Mitra then questioned the player's commitment to the club and to the game.

The Jalpaiguri match was neither an international one nor part of a recognized tournament. The club could have spoken to him if he missed trainings but instead, it gave the impression that football clubs are nothing but fiefdoms.

Even former Bagan coach Karim Bencharifa had not been consulted before the letter was issued to the player. The Moroccan, however, did not want to comment on the issue and said that it would not be right on his part to say anything since the battle was between Bagan and the player. Interestingly, Mitra, a chartered accountant by profession, did confirm that although Baichung had been show-caused for reasons related to football, the coach had not been involved in this decision. This is not an uncommon practice in Indian clubs, where officials usually override coaches.

Though Baichung missed a few training sessions, his commitment to the club was never in doubt. Some of the rehearsals were even held in Calcutta, and Sonia travelled there a couple of times to accommodate Baichung's football schedule.

However, things got complicated once Baichung survived the initial rounds and had to rush from Calcutta to Mumbai more often than the Bagan members had anticipated. This resulted in Baichung missing more training sessions than expected. 'They could have spoken to me. Instead, they show-caused me and the media got involved. It just shows how poorly things get managed in Indian clubs,' he rued.

Baichung's stint in Bagan—he joined the club on 15 June, 2006—was supposed to be the high point of his career. Whenever he changed clubs, it earned immediate attention from the media and the football community. He was still a rage in Indian football then and held his own against all odds. In Bagan, he formed an enviable attacking pair with Brazilian striker Ramirez Barreto. As one of the biggest stars in Indian football, Baichung was expected to take the green-and-maroon club to new heights.

However, the 2006–07 season turned out to be dismal for both Bagan and Baichung as the Calcutta club finished eighth in the NFL. In the next season, he regained his form and confidence and started to score again. His predatory skills, which made him one of India's star strikers, was applauded once again as he helped Bagan finish fourth in the I-League, scoring ten goals in eighteen matches. He also won the Indian Player of the Year award for the second time in 2008.

In the 2008–09 season, despite a ten-match winning streak in the I-League, Bagan could only finish second behind Churchill Brothers. They lost to the now disbanded Mahindra United on the last day of the League, but Baichung finished the season with six goals.

'After I joined *Jhalak* in February 2009, the first game we played was against Chirag United and I scored two goals. We beat I-League champions Dempo Sports Club in the Super Cup in Gurgaon where I scored a hat-trick. In the two AFC Cup games which Bagan lost, the opponent coaches praised my performance,' he recalled.

More drama unfolded when the then Indian coach and one of Baichung's ardent supporters, Bob Houghton, jumped in to back his favourite player. The Englishman who coached the Indian team between 2006 and 2011 described Bagan's attempt to publicly humiliate the star player as 'inane'.

On 22 June, 2009, Baichung signed a one-year contract with East Bengal. It was perceived as a move that challenged the rules and forced the Indian Football Association, the parent body of West Bengal football, to take a decision on his suspension even as Bagan called the signing a 'farce'. Till the time of signing with East Bengal, Baichung was under suspension and had a year left with Bagan.

However, Baichung said that the Bagan agreement was only a memorandum of understanding (MoU) and not a contract as there was no mention of any advance payment. He also said that his participation in *Jhalak* was not the reason for his suspension as the club took action two and a half months after he first appeared on the show.

'They never objected or complained when I started going for rehearsals in Mumbai in February. It all started when I skipped an exhibition match at Jalpaiguri, which was at the end of the season,' he said.

Show-cause notice

On 8 June, when Bagan slapped him with a six-month suspension, it was then that Baichung decided to challenge it through his lawyer, Usha Nath Banerjee.

Baichung did not reply to the show-cause notice and in a media conference on the eve of Bagan's AFC Cup match in Calcutta on 18 May, 2009, he stunned everyone when he announced that he would quit the club because his commitment had been questioned. He felt he was being targeted by a section of club officials who did not approve of his participation in the dance show.

Bagan, infamous for its faction rivalry, then went on to blame Baichung for the club's unimpressive show in the I-League. Things were fine at first, when Bagan had won a record ten games in India's premier event. They only started to stumble after they were thrashed 3–0 by rivals East Bengal.

His legal counsel contended that Bagan's show-cause notice to Baichung was illegal and argued that the suspension on his client could not be sustained on factual and legal grounds, and that the club had failed to follow proper procedure. Banerjee cited Article 22A(a) of the IFA's constitution, which clearly states that an affiliated unit may suspend or ban a player registered under the IFA only after initiating disciplinary proceedings and providing reasonable opportunity to the player in question of being heard. But none of this was adhered to before the suspension order was handed to Baichung.

Banerjee went on to add that the letter served to Baichung by Bagan on 14 May, 2009, seeking clarification for his absence from the practice sessions before the important I-League matches and from the exhibition match at Jalpaiguri, wasn't a show-cause letter. It was merely a letter seeking clarification. Moreover, Baichung had already stated in his letter dated 21 May, 2009, that he had sought permission from the club for leave, a claim that Bagan did not refute in their suspension letter. This only proved that Baichung had taken club's permission to attend the show.

This was no ordinary battle as it was fought between Mohun Bagan, one of India's leading clubs, and Baichung, an icon of Indian football. In the end, it was merely an ego fight as both parties claimed they were right in their decisions.

Calcutta clubs like Bengal's Marxist leaders

Bagan's inappropriate conduct virtually turned everyone in Indian football against them. The way the club chased down the best of Indian footballers was something nobody appreciated. Most of Baichung's India teammates believed that the club was wrong and should have contacted him before taking any action.

'He is by far the most well-known Indian footballer outside India,' commented Steve Darby. An Englishman, Darby was Bryan Robson's assistant with the Thailand national team between 2009 and 2011 and is a well-known analyst on ESPN-Star Sports. Based in Vietnam, the 58-year-old coach has an excellent understanding of Asian players. 'Indian football is very self-centred and the club officials think the world follows their game. Sadly, it doesn't. India needs icons like Baichung to take the game to the outside world,' he said.

Darby once famously said, with regard to Bagan, that a chartered accountant (Mitra) and an advocate (Tutu Bose, the club president) don't understand football. He also suggested that Bagan introspect on why it had allowed one of its most important players to participate in a reality show at a time when the club was fighting for the I-League title and the AFC Cup. This belies logic even to this day.

Bagan's show-cause notice seems no more than Mitra's personal attack on the player. Had the club officials been serious about their claims, they could or would have reprimanded him the very day that Bagan took on Al Wehdat in their AFC Cup tie in Jordan. But surprisingly, the club kept quiet and decided to take action against him only after he refused to play in the exhibition match at the end of the season.

It wouldn't be too far-fetched to compare the Calcutta clubs, including Bagan, to the erstwhile Marxist government in their state—both refuse to change their mindset and embrace professionalism. Even a decade back, most clubs would sign rookie players on a plain sheet of paper as there would be no formal contracts. Most players who came from far-flung areas of rural Bengal would have no option but to agree to the promises because, for them, a chance to play for one of the big clubs would be a dream fulfilled.

In the history of the sport there have been numerous face-offs between players and clubs. But in India, it's the glaring lack of professionalism among the officials who wield enormous power that has led to unavoidable court battles. When Baichung had first expressed interest in the dance show, Bagan could have told him right then about their principles and guidelines. The club could also have stopped him from attending his first rehearsal in February. Why they chose to break their silence only in April is anyone's guess.

After Bagan appealed to the AIFF the same year to seek their intervention, Baichung's travel to Delhi became a routine affair as the case was tabled in front of the national body's Players' Status Committee. Surprisingly, they too failed to decide on the matter as one member refused to give his opinion. This became a pressing affair at the national federation office at

Dwarka, Delhi, as the AIFF wanted to resolve the issue at the earliest.

Almost every week, meetings involving Baichung and officials of Mohun Bagan and the AIFF were held either at the federation headquarters or at the ministry office of the then civil and aviation minister, Praful Patel, who was the acting president of AIFF.

But those meetings failed to accomplish much; the club was adamant on imposing a six-month suspension on Baichung, who had already signed up with East Bengal. The then Indian coach, Houghton, in turn, criticized the Bagan officials for asking the former national skipper to attend the meeting ahead of the 2009 Nehru Cup final.

As AIFF failed to arrive at a solution, its executive committee decided to refer the matter to an arbitrator on 30 August, 2009. Senior advocate and former additional solicitor general of India Amarendra Sharan was thus appointed on 3 September, 2009, and he issued notices to Bagan and Baichung two days later. Bagan was represented by the Delhi-based legal firm Suri & Company.

During the five rounds of hearings, Baichung moved an application pleading for interim relief so that he could play for East Bengal, while Bagan contended that the proceedings before Sharan were a conciliatory process and not arbitration.

At that point, Baichung, always a non-controversial figure, said that he had become disoriented and lost faith in the club after the show-cause notice had been released to the media.

'I had told Bagan to release me and suggested that we should part on good terms even though my contract had another year to go. I didn't understand why they wanted to keep me after all this,' Baichung said.

After many arguments and counter-arguments between him and the club, Baichung finally heaved a sigh of relief on 26 September, 2009, when Sharan granted him temporary relief to play for the club of his choice. Even the FIFA laws stipulate that a club cannot hold back a player from playing unless there are serious charges levied against him.

Many insiders in the AIFF felt that the charges against him weren't serious. Besides, the club's relation with the national body had never been cordial. Naturally, there was a concerted effort to defend the national team captain.

Support from the North-east

While the controversy was unfolding, the dance show progressed to the grand finale and the trophy seemed well within Baichung's reach. He may not have been in the best frame of mind, but Baichung was always known for pulling it off when the chips were down. He never fell short of support during this rough patch—neither from his dancing partner and choreographer Sonia, nor from the North-eastern states which rallied behind the player. Social organizations and football clubs backed him too. Hence, while his own club, Bagan, disapproved of his dancing and banned him, Baichung's popularity soared. In fact, Bagan's negative publicity helped

Baichung garner support even from the non-footballing communities who wanted him to win.

Citizens Forum, a social organization led by former Sikkim minister Thukchuk Lachungpa and supported by Gangtok-based local cable network Nayuma Television, and by organizations like the Tibetan Youth Club, bought vouchers worth Rs 150,000 to vote for Baichung. They had meetings with representatives of a popular local club, Prashant Fan Club, in Darjeeling and Kalimpong, and started a campaign in the North-east to support the footballer.

Various football associations in Calcutta, Sikkim and across the country also voted for him. A mass voting event was held at Hotel Himalayan Heights in Gangtok where people voted through SMSes, using the recharge coupons provided by Citizens Forum. The North-east was bent on seeing Baichung win the show.

'As someone who loves dance, I saw this as a once-in-a-lifetime opportunity to experience something different. It was great and challenging. Regardless of what sport you play or what you do, if you love dance, you should be part of something like this,' he said with a smile.

As his fans in Sikkim say about his *Jhalak* campaign, '*Ki ki so so iha gyalo* (good will triumph over evil).'

7

An Idealist Leader

When Baichung Bhutia said yes to Mamata Banerjee's request that he contest the 2014 Lok Sabha polls from Darjeeling, many eyebrows were raised. It seemed to me that he deserved a better deal from the ruling Trinamool Congress party in West Bengal, a state that became his second home during his professional career from 1993–95 and again from 2002–11. He not only made Calcutta the centre of his professional life, he also carried the City of Joy in his heart wherever he went. One would have thought the former footballer would have been nominated for the Upper House in Parliament, but instead he was handed the difficult constituency of Darjeeling, where the ruling party's political equation with the TMC is fraught and complex.

It was a tall order for Baichung; even poll experts didn't expect him to win the seat, knowing the TMC would have to fight the election without the support of the Gorkha Janmukti Morcha, the top regional party in the hills. As it turned out, the former footballer was beaten by BJP candidate S.S. Ahluwalia by 4.91 lakh votes.

Initially, Baichung didn't want to contest the election and was in two minds when Didi approached him in December 2013. Eventually, he agreed as he couldn't turn down 'Ms Banerjee's request'.

Though his critics called him 'ambitious' for contesting the polls, I felt it was a wise decision, knowing that Baichung's promise to work for the betterment of the hills was sincere.

I spoke to Baichung the day after the election results and he seemed unruffled. Perhaps he was mentally prepared for the outcome of the polls.

Baichung has carved a place for himself as a dynamic sports personality and I doubt if, after retirement, he ever actively thought about adding another feather—of becoming a political leader—to his cap. It was his leadership quality that prompted the West Bengal chief minister to encourage him to try his luck in an untested territory like the Lok Sabha elections, and her request which made him agree to do so.

Baichung has always been at the forefront when it comes to doing something constructive for the people, be it for the sport or for society at large. When a major earthquake hit Sikkim in 2011, Baichung swung into action, involving various charities and helping raise funds for his state.

If empowerment, encouragement, vision, and values are what make a true leader, then Baichung fits the bill perfectly. Even though he is no longer an active participant in the sport, developing football in India remains his top priority.

Bold and determined

In India, not too many public figures speak out in support of controversial issues, especially if those are of a political nature. This again, is one aspect where Baichung stands out. Taking a stand for a cause close to his heart—Tibet—he startled the sports community by boldly pulling out of the 2008 Beijing Olympics torch relay which passed through New Delhi on 17 April. The icon didn't care much about the repercussions of his refusal to carry the Olympic torch because he wanted to speak his mind against Chinese oppression in Tibet. 'It was a completely personal decision based on my feelings,' he said.

He has never been one to wear his emotions on his sleeve but this is one issue where he shows complete solidarity with Tibetans fighting against Chinese rule. His refusal to carry the Olympic torch was a mark of protest. His decision earned him the support and admiration of the Tibetan community in India. The Tibetan spiritual leader, the Dalai Lama, has lived in India since 1959—the year he fled his homeland following the Chinese occupation—and India is home to more than 150,000 Tibetan exiles.

Less than five months before the opening ceremony in Beijing, Tibet's government-in-exile, which is based in India, had said that 140 people had been killed in a crackdown by Chinese security forces during anti-China protests. It was this incident that incensed Baichung and prompted his decision.

Baichung's own state, Sikkim, has long been claimed by China as its own territory.

Buddhist by birth, the former India captain defended his decision, adding that he disapproved of any kind of violence. He also felt that the issue of not carrying the Olympic torch was blown out of proportion. 'I sympathize with the Tibetan cause and I stand by the Tibetan people in their fight,' said Baichung, whose ancestors were Tibetans.

Baichung's support for the Tibetan cause has an interesting parallel with boxing legend Muhammad Ali's protest against the Vietnam War. Arguably the best sportsman of the century, Ali earned the wrath of the US administration when, in 1967, he refused to join the armed forces because he opposed the Vietnam War. His words—'No, I'm not going 10,000 miles from home to help murder and burn another poor nation simply to continue the domination of white slave masters of the darker people the world over'—are hailed as one of the boldest statements ever made by a leading sportsperson against the US government. His boxing license was withdrawn and he was denied a place in the boxing fraternity. He was also given a five-year jail term and a $10,000 fine. Though he remained out of prison on bail, he was stripped of his passport and his heavyweight title and banned from boxing in the US. Ali returned to boxing in 1970 and his conviction was reversed in 1971.

Ali's courage and determination are rare in the annals of sporting history. He showed the world that he cared more about his values and beliefs than about his career or reputation. This display of solidarity won him love and respect from around the world. Baichung's act of courage, however, was strongly criticized by some Indian sportsmen.

'Baichung is often described as the Indian David Beckham for his commitment to the game, his skill, and good looks. The veteran is also that rare breed: a politically minded footballer,' said CNN's James Montague during India's 2011 Asian Cup campaign in Doha.

Those who know Baichung from close quarters will be well acquainted with his ability to stand his ground and speak his mind without mincing words. Not surprisingly, he sends his team, United Sikkim FC, to the annual Gyalyum Chemo Memorial Gold Cup football tournament, which is organized by the Tibetan Sports Association in memory of the late mother of His Holiness the XIV Dalai Lama, and has often turned up as a guest at the event since its inception in 1981.

'I look up to His Holiness because I admire his concept of non-violence,' he said. 'It wasn't right for me to carry the torch. I never tried to mix sports with politics but I have some friends who're fighting for human rights in Tibet. That's why I didn't want to carry the torch,' he said, explaining his stand on Tibet.

Baichung is not simply a star footballer or a celebrity. He is seen as a representative of India's North-eastern states, which are often unfortunately sidelined. He evokes the kind of hero worship that many stars would envy. Parents in Sikkim narrate to their kids the inspirational story of a boy from a nondescript village who overcame numerous hardships and shot to stardom.

'I always wanted to do something for the North-east—not just for Sikkim,' he said. 'Living up to the expectations of my fans and the people of the North-east is not a burden—it is a great honour to represent their identity. Many people from Manipur, Mizoram, Sikkim, Nagaland, and Meghalaya do not venture out of their towns because they feel out of place in mainland India. We want to identify ourselves with the rest of India. We didn't have political or corporate leaders from the North-east. But in the past decade or so, sport has given much hope to the people. Football is a big deal in the North-east, and achievements in this sport have given hope to the people of this region. So, it was important for someone from this region to come out and make a mark for himself and his people,' he said.

In fact, after his emergence as football's leading star, other athletes from the region have been motivated to come to the fore, going on to represent India in the Olympics, Asian Games, and other international events. From boxers Dingko Singh and Mary Kom, and tennis player Somdev Devvarman to archer Bombayla Devi, the number of sportspersons from the North-east representing the country in international events has steadily increased.

Indian football's golden years

The golden period of Indian football started in 1948 and ended in 1962, during which the team competed in four Olympic Games, including a semifinal outing in the 1956 Melbourne Games. The team also won two gold medals in the 1951 and 1962 Asian Games, and their last notable international success was achieved in the 1970 Asian Games in Bangkok, where they won a bronze medal. But today, even though FIFA considers India a 'sleeping giant', Indian football has not been able to impress at the level of Asian and world tournaments. After forty-four years, the bronze won at Bangkok still stands as the lone success and our world ranking is 154—below the strife-torn Afghanistan even—which is proof enough of the poor development that has taken place at the grass-roots level.

Without international success, it naturally becomes difficult to motivate and encourage a team. Nehru Cup, India's only international football tournament, was started in 1982 in Calcutta where, throughout the 1980s, Indian teams came a cropper against the top European and Latin American teams that played in India with some of their biggest World Cup stars of that era.

In the 1980s India had some brilliant players like Prasun Banerjee, Prasanto Banerjee, Sudip Chatterjee, Krishanu Dey, Shabbir Ali, Bhaskar Ganguly, Babu Mani and others. The team also had a great tactician in coach Ćirić Milovan, but it lacked a leader. India never finished on the podium and won no laurels except plaudits for their 'brilliant' games against the heavyweights.

Baichung had his job cut out as a leader—motivating his teammates and helping them banish the thought that they were mere pushovers. The degree to which he was able to accomplish this is admirable.

Under his leadership, India won their maiden Nehru Cup in 2007 and retained the title in 2009 in Delhi's Ambedkar Stadium. Though the success came against the West and South Asian teams, it nevertheless bolstered the players' spirit and confidence.

'Throughout my career, I've seen and felt the frustration of my teammates, particularly after foreign tours when they see the kind of training facilities available outside India.'

Their tepid popularity in their own country does not help either. While Indian youngsters religiously follow the best foreign football leagues, they hardly show any interest in Indian tournaments, particularly the I-League. Baichung agrees. So how do we raise the standard of football in India and, in turn, boost its popularity within the country, I ask him.

'To produce good players, we need to have very good infrastructure. But this support system is not there in India. When they're seventeen or eighteen, young players don't get access to even basic training or youth development programmes,' he said.

Emerging leader

During the transition period of Indian football in the first few years of the new millennium, when many senior players retired, Baichung was seen as the emerging leader, ahead of most of his peers, including Renedy, with whom he has always shared great understanding. Therefore, he was naturally chosen by both Indian and foreign coaches as the leader, motivator, and guide to his team.

At the club level too, Baichung commanded the respect of his teammates, officials, and fans. Surprisingly, while Mohun Bagan made him their captain in 2007–08, in East Bengal he was only the stand-in captain as the club has a policy of handing over the captain's armband only to those who have played for them at a stretch. Baichung had left the club first in 1995–96, then in 1999–2000 and finally in the 2003–05 season.

'As a leader, he had charisma. Most of his Indian teammates admired him for his leadership qualities and also because he was glamorous,' said his friend Sherap. 'Whether it was his Armani suit or his Audi car, his juniors were in awe of his style. He had earned every bit of his fame from the game. But despite all this, he remained a leader who never bragged,' he added.

At parties and get-togethers, I have seen him surrounded by his young teammates, the centre of attention. Interestingly, I've also noticed a small group of junior players from Bengal seemingly reluctant to approach him. As a star who spoke in English and Hindi, listened to Western music, and was not averse to shaking a leg on stage, he evoked admiration. But as a team leader, he could put anyone—from a newcomer to a veteran—at ease.

'I remember shooting a promotional film with the national team in Delhi's Le Meridian hotel. Baichung was very friendly with the entire team and never behaved like a snooty senior. He was like a helpful and concerned elder brother to most of his teammates,' said Prerna Raghav, head of creative strategy, Branded Content, Times Television Network.

Freedom of expression

Baichung's success as a leader and mentor provides a contrast to that of Sachin Tendulkar, the cricket legend. Tendulkar's two brief spells as Indian captain in the late 1990s were mostly unsuccessful despite his brilliant record as a player. However, in cricket the role of the captain has more significance than in football, where the manager or coach has greater control on the team from a technical perspective. In the football rulebook, currently up on FIFA's website, the football captain is mentioned only thrice.

In fact, the rules explicitly state: 'The captain of a team has no special status or privileges under the Laws of the Game but he has a degree of responsibility for the behavior of his team.' And, sometimes the behaviour of the team can be hostile, even dangerous, in football.

To measure Baichung's achievement as a leader, one has to study the Indian teams he led, which had players from the North-east, Maharashtra, Goa, Kerala, Punjab and Bengal—states with vastly different cultures, cuisine, languages and beliefs. Yet Baichung remained the unifying factor, leading his teams to two Nehru Cup wins and an AFC Challenge Cup title between 2007 and 2009.

Before his time, the national team's wins and losses hardly received any media attention, but Baichung changed all that. 'The players don't speak out against injustice. They keep quiet because their humble backgrounds do not allow them to go and revolt against the associations and officials. Also, they are scared about the repercussions,' he explained.

In the 1970s and 80s, when the Indian team was dominated by Bengali players, there were reports of friction between the Bengalis and players from other states, like Punjab, Kerala, and Goa. These teams traditionally had Bengalis in the positions of coach and manager, and no long-term captain. It was only during the coaching tenure of the late Milovan in the mid-1980s that a rotation policy was introduced for the captain's armband.

With Baichung on board, the Indian team got a new dimension as most of the coaches appreciated his ideas. He displayed a certain élan and sophistication that finally drew media attention to the reticent Indian footballers. When Stephen Constantine joined the team as coach in 2002, he had no hesitation in choosing him as the captain. Other coaches who came after Constantine, too, recognized Baichung's popularity in the country. Naturally, none of them made any attempt to displace him from the hot seat.

Not surprisingly, the Indian team enjoyed their best years from 2006–09 in an era of liberalism under Englishman Bob Houghton who had a great equation with Baichung. The two of them worked in tandem to ensure that every player gave his best for Team India, but still enjoyed his freedom off the field. There was no gag order or movement restriction imposed on the players. This worked well and India won their first Nehru Cup in 2007, and successfully defended the title two years later at the same venue.

'We played for the team. We won for the team. There was no individual performance. I always put it down to the players that the team comes first,' added Baichung.

Baichung was hailed as the undisputed leader by the entire nation that started following the fortunes of a success-starved football team for the first time after the 2007 Nehru Cup win. He was a spokesperson, moderator, friend, guide, brother and a big-hearted skipper who ensured that everybody got a fair deal. Apart from Sikkimese and Nepali, he also spoke in Bengali, Hindi and English, which made it a lot easier for him to connect with his teammates, exchanging ideas and sharing his vision for Team India.

'I captained India for eleven years, but wasn't a natural leader from the start. As captain I had to perform on the field to be able to earn the respect of my teammates,' he explained.

Under his captaincy, India won the LG Cup in Vietnam in 2002, the SAFF championships thrice, two Nehru Cup titles and the 2008 AFC Challenge Cup which assured the team a place in the 2011 Asian Cup in Qatar.

Like other kids of his generation, Sunil Chhetri, too, grew up watching Baichung play. So when his role model and mentor retired, Chhetri was chosen to replace him. Barring Chhetri, very few next-generation players have made such a strong impression. This Delhi boy was ahead of the rest when it came to filling Baichung's shoes. Performance was the only way of convincing the coach and co-players about his calibre as a leader. Chhetri is a true reflection of Baichung's halcyon days and he scored plenty of stellar goals before beating Baichung's 42-goal record in a match against Nepal last year in Siliguri.

'I remain thankful to him. He has guided me to become what I am today,' said the current Indian skipper.

To see for myself how Baichung's home state worshipped him, I took a 45-minute drive with him from Tinkitam to Namchi, where the Sikkim government built a stadium in 2001 and named it after him. We walked in through a pagoda-like entrance inscribed with the words 'Baichung Bhutia Stadium'. He is the first player to have been given this honour while still in his heyday. The venue serves as a reminder to posterity about Baichung's contribution to the game in India. Not even Sachin Tendulkar had a stadium named after him at a time when he dominated international cricket.

I was a tad surprised to step into a grassless stadium as we took a round of the grounds. It was like a dust bowl with concrete stands on one side. 'Now you understand how much our players struggle,' he told me wryly.

After having played on the best of football pitches across England, it must have been all the more painful to see the pathetic condition of stadiums in his own country. No wonder then, that he has always called for better infrastructure for the growth of the game.

In 2000, while on a summer break in India from Bury FC, he floated the idea of forming a players' association. He may have ruffled a few feathers, but nobody spoke against it as he was the only shining star of the game. In fact, all the players backed him. His success on the field allowed him to voice the concerns and needs of players who got a rough deal from their clubs and the national federation.

The Football Players Association of India (FPAI) was formed on 28 June, 2006 as a registered society. Under Baichung's leadership, FPAI was modelled as an association by the players, of the players, and for the players. It is the exclusive representative body and collective bargaining agent for India's professional footballers. Since 2008, it has also been a member association of FIFPro, the world body for players, and a partner of FIFA. Last November, Baichung was selected to serve on the technical committee of FIFPro for a term of four years, becoming the only representative from Asia on the six-member committee alongside three members from Europe and one each from Africa and South America.

'FPAI is committed to ensuring that each and every professional player in India is treated equally no matter which club, state or team he is playing in,' said Baichung, who handed over the FPAI mantle to Renedy this year.

The FPAI assists players in negotiating contracts with both clubs and associations, and federation teams. The essence of negotiation is no longer just the financial rewards but includes other terms and conditions, such as the length of the contract, insurance coverage, work-related injuries, accommodation, and other incentives.

FIFPro, the sole international representative body for professional football players around the world, has pledged to support the FPAI in its initiatives towards the growth and welfare of Indian footballers. The FPAI also has a seat in the Board of FIFPro Division Asia. Under Baichung's leadership, the FPAI has been encouraging young players through an annual awards ceremony, which is an opportunity to honour the footballers and entertain them as they mingle with celebrities, other players, their families, and all stakeholders.

One would be hard pressed to find another icon from the sport who has associated himself so deeply with the promotion of football in the country. Chuni Goswami, one of India's biggest icons, enjoyed his retired life as an adviser to the West Bengal Sports Council and the TFA. The last time I saw him, he was managing a nursing home owned by his son in east Calcutta. Another stalwart, P.K., known for his loquacity, coached a few clubs and later, the TFA, after he relinquished his job with the Eastern Railways.

Trendsetter

Baichung remains a trendsetter. He has proved his mettle by contributing constructively to football, rather than just confining himself to media interviews, social gatherings, and cutting ribbons at puja pandals.

'What I respect tremendously is the fact that he had the courage and the moral values to establish the FPAI. Without him, the FPAI wouldn't have survived or even taken off. He had the courage to fight some of the inane regulations he came up against, and led the way for the Indian players. This, to me, will be his greatest legacy,' said Steve Darby.

'As a player and leader, his contribution is immense. He is the best by my book and I think it will be a long time before a player of his stature is found again,' said I.M. Vijayan.

His home state association, SFA, also found him a tough nut to crack when Baichung demanded that the local football clubs be involved in the functioning of the association. He was upset when SFA ignored the demands of Sikkimese clubs. Assured of the clubs' unwavering support, Baichung formed the Football Club Association of Sikkim (FCAS) which now works for the welfare of players and clubs in Sikkim.

Among other demands, the FCAS had sought that two members of all clubs that have played in Senior Division S-League for a minimum of five years be given permanent membership with voting rights in the SFA and two FCAS executive members be made executive members of SFA as well.

Another demand of the FCAS was that clubs from within and around Gangtok playing in S-League and Independence Day tournaments be given Rs 5000 per match by the organizing committee, and all outstation teams be given taxi fares in addition to Rs 5000.

Baichung has left no stone unturned in order to improve football at the grass-roots level. However, United Sikkim is not just about the battles on and off the field. It is also about the people of a small state—tucked away in the Himalayas and sharing international boundaries with three countries—getting an opportunity to stamp their presence on the national consciousness.

Sikkim became an Indian state in 1975, just over a year before Baichung was born. Coming from such a young state, United Sikkim will always enjoy one thing that few football clubs in India do—a loyal support base.

'The USFC gave us a chance to play in the I-League,' says Mobin Rai, a United Sikkim player. The defender is a product of the Sikkim Sports Academy. Today United Sikkim FC has at least a dozen home-based players who are happy to play for the club just because of Baichung.

A devoted and sincere sportsman, Baichung argued in favour of a Sports Bill as he, like most other players, was disillusioned with the way the numerous federations in the country have been functioning. When the International Olympic Committee decided to suspend India from world sports last year, Baichung urged the Indian body to amend its constitution in accordance with the Olympic Charter.

Coming specifically to football, isn't it strange that a country with a 100-year-old history in the sport took so long to start a national league? As Baichung correctly puts it, 'It's the lack of knowledge. We need people who have knowledge to show us the way.'

Even with so many responsibilities, dreams and hard battles to wage, Baichung has remained immensely likeable, an unassuming star who always has a smile on his face.

After the earthquake in Sikkim in 2011, Baichung chipped in to support the people of his state. With the help of the state government, he organized charity matches to raise funds. He brought in football legends like Ruud Gullit and Christian Karembeu, world motorsports champion Tim Tranker, Scorpions guitarist Rudolf Schenker, and actors Rahul Bose and Neha Dhupia, to participate in his fundraising match.

I've met and conversed with sports legends Diego Maradona, Boris Becker, Nadia Comaneci, Mark Spitz, and Michael Johnson and all of them had one thing in common: they did not want to fade into oblivion once they hung up their boots. They all want to travel around the world to support their sport, fight for a cause, and engage themselves in charity work.

It's for similar reasons that Baichung, too, keeps himself occupied serving the game and society. His family says he is rarely in his Gangtok home, busy as he is with his many commitments. Baichung believes that every individual has a commitment towards society, and he is working hard to fulfil his own.

Fame hasn't changed this celebrity. You would still find him awaiting his turn in queues or walking down the streets just like anyone else. And therein may lie the secret to his popularity.

8

End of an Era

On 24 August, 2011, a week before Lionel Messi played a friendly game against Venezuela in Calcutta, the star of modern Indian football walked into the sunset.

Dressed casually in a grey T-shirt and jeans, Baichung walked into the conference room of Football House in Dwarka to announce his retirement. Baichung had been a part of our lives since 1993, winning young and old hearts alike with his skill and charm. Rarely had the news of a retirement in Indian football garnered so much publicity. His retirement made us feel strangely empty. And old.

Playing for Sikkim United against Sesa Goa in a Durand Cup preliminary group match in Delhi two months before hanging up his boots, Baichung proved that he still had his unique touch. He had not lost his knack of darting towards the goal at just the right moment. Yet, it was also evident that he no longer had his old mobility and his signature speed.

In his later years, Baichung had his share of lacklustre moments and there were murmurs that he had morphed into a brand. Many football observers were unwittingly harsh, referring to him in past tense even before his official retirement.

Baichung, however, has always remained poised and cool, never letting emotions overpower him. But his parting speech was an emotional one. Even the most stoic turn emotional when they leave the game they once dominated and that evening Baichung was no different. He did smile as he bade farewell, but one could see the tumult of emotions on his face. It had been a long and memorable journey since he first donned the India colours and went out against Thailand as a substitute in the 1995 Nehru Cup in Calcutta.

Baichung first thought about retirement in 2008 when India won the AFC Challenge Cup amidst an unexpectedly late monsoon in Delhi in September, thereby earning a berth in the 2011 Asian Cup.

In the line of fire

'I thought of calling it a day after winning the AFC Challenge Cup in 2008. But after India won the Cup and qualified for the 2011 Asian Cup, I wanted to do it during the mega event in Doha,' he said.

However, things didn't proceed as planned and he was plagued by injury throughout 2009. That year, he became the only footballer to be honoured with the Padma Shri during his playing career. But injury had slowed his pace and he missed club matches for East Bengal who faced an ignominious 5–3 drubbing against Mohun Bagan in the I-League, with Baichung helplessly watching from the dugouts. There were feeble whispers about his slide in form, while critics raised doubts about his fitness. A niggling calf-muscle injury continued to trouble him and, between September 2010 and January 2011, he was unable to play a single full match. Just before the Asian Cup in Doha, he flew to Chennai to consult sports medicine expert Dr Kannan Pugazendhi for his injury.

Renedy said that he didn't want him to retire on a sour note. 'He was frustrated with his injury. His calf muscle was refusing to take any more pressure. I've rarely seen him so disturbed,' said Renedy.

In mid-2009, Baichung found himself in an acrimonious fight with his club Mohun Bagan when he missed a few friendly and practice matches owing to his appearance in the dance reality show *Jhalak Dikhhla Jaa*.

In the midst of it all, as the Nehru Cup approached, he prepared himself to reprise India's 2007 win. Leading the team of defending champions, Baichung put up an impressive performance and India retained the title in 2009. In fact, his three-goal feat and enterprising leadership earned him the title of Player of the Tournament. In the same tournament, he played and scored in his 100th international match against Kyrgyzstan. It was enough to silence the naysayers.

In the last three years of his career, Baichung was also criticized for donning the dual role of player and entrepreneur when he planned to launch his own football club.

If age had slowed down his pace, recurring injuries had disoriented him. His inclusion in the 2011 Asian Cup squad kicked up a row in some quarters. His critics alleged that he had used his influence to retain his place in the national team and promote his own club.

Among his critics was the then Indian team manager, Pradeep Chowdhury, who had a spat over Baichung with coach Bob Houghton. Chowdhury quit the team in Dubai, a few weeks before it left for Doha, the venue of the tournament. He argued that since Baichung was injured, he should be replaced by a fit player. He also blamed Baichung for using his influence and charm to stay with the national team on the AIFF's expenses. This time too, Houghton turned out to be Baichung's saviour and stoutly defended his decision to include him in the squad.

Chowdhury was not alone in his tirade against Baichung. There were veiled protests from some of his teammates who doubted their captain's fitness level and questioned why he had been chosen instead of a fit player. However, it wasn't clear why Chowdhury didn't raise the issue till the team landed in Dubai. After all, Baichung had been down with injuries much before the team had been selected.

Some observers compared Baichung with Sachin Tendulkar, who, too, had delayed his retirement. A debate erupted over whether Baichung was blocking the way for youngsters in the team.

Unfazed in the line of fire, Houghton and the AIFF backed their skipper and felt that it was an opportunity for him to bring down the curtains at the continental championship where India was playing after twenty-seven years. In fact, Houghton maintained that he had no second thoughts about including him in his twenty-three-member squad for the 2011 Asian Cup.

Asian Cup campaign

In his interviews Houghton maintained his staunch support for Baichung. The coach believed that Baichung deserved to retire in a blaze of glory. Anything less than such a stage would be tantamount to belittling the star's contribution to Indian football.

Many fans believe that Houghton was right from a purely sentimental point of view—Baichung did deserve to play alongside some of the biggest stars in the world, including Park Ji-Sung, then captain of the South Korean team, Manchester United star Shinji Kagawa, Keisuke Honda of Japan and a few English Premier League-returned Aussies.

In a dramatic turn of events, however, the injury-prone striker was dropped from the squad ahead of India's first match against Australia, registered as an official, and then brought back as a player. The problem was that only twenty-three players could be registered as a team in the tournament. Since

Baichung was injured, he was accommodated as 'coaching staff' because Houghton felt his mere presence in the dugouts would be enough to boost the team's morale.

In the opening fixture against the Socceroos at the fabulous Al Sadd Stadium, Baichung found himself in the reserves as he wasn't fit. The Aussies hammered India 4–0. He was rested again in the second match against Bahrain, where India lost 5–2. The media back home argued that if his inclusion had been a logical decision, then why was he spending all his time in the dugouts as a member of the staff?

Houghton didn't introduce Baichung when India dominated the ten-member Bahrain team in the latter half, after Faouzi Ayesh received his second yellow card. Though it is debatable how much Baichung could have contributed, his presence would have spurred his teammates on. India had already got off to a great start, cancelling out Bahrain's 8th-minute goal with a goal by Gouramangi a minute later. But Houghton's insistence to start every match with central midfielders Climax Lawrence, who wore the captain's armband, and N.P. Pradeep, who was taken off in the 74th minute, was baffling as both of them were unfit and visibly struggled.

Houghton's decisions and the inclusion of unfit players in the team drew flak from all corners. He needlessly banked on them and, surprisingly, kept his faith in most of them, including Baichung. Samir Naik and N.S. Manju suffered from poor fitness much before the tournament, yet Houghton didn't choose to include a fitter left-back. India was left with two makeshift left-backs, Syed Rahim Nabi and Dipak Mondol, who, however, were more comfortable in defensive duties. This resulted in an incredibly weak left flank.

Houghton was stubborn in his belief that he had put together a strong team. At his behest, a pool of thirty players, including Subrata Paul, Renedy, Nabi, Clifford Miranda and Abhishek Yadav, were contracted with AIFF for the 2011 Asian Cup. But when India lost miserably in the friendlies in Dubai, which preceded the mega event in Doha, the selection of some of these players was questioned.

India had already bowed out of the tournament after the defeats against Australia and Bahrain. It remained to be seen if Houghton would give Baichung a chance to don the national colours in a major event like the Asian Cup. The Indian media was abuzz: would Baichung be part of this tournament for the last time?

At Al Wakrah, on the outskirts of Doha, when Baichung came on the field at the team's training session, it was clear that he would finally play against South Korea. Under the blazing sun, he ran full stretch, dabbled with the ball and even took some cracking shots at the goal in the hour-long practice session. He was finally fit to play against the Koreans in what would become his last international appearance.

At the South Korean team's practice sessions, I casually asked one of their visiting journalists if he would know, by any chance, the names of any Indian players.

'There is someone called "Butia" in your team. He looks very much like us. Is he Indian? We've heard he's good but injured,' said the Korean journalist.

Final 15 minutes

It was an overcast and chilly evening on 18 January at the Al Gharafa Stadium in Doha. Minutes before kick-off there was a light drizzle. But unlike Indian football fields, the pitch did not get slushy and there were no mud patches on the players' shirts.

Expectedly, the mighty Koreans had already taken an unassailable 3–1 lead by the 23rd minute. India's emerging star Sunil Chhetri found the net once, courtesy a spot-kick in the 12th minute. Houghton and his boys knew that their Asian Cup sojourn was over for good. But the English coach wanted India's favourite player to be on the field for at least a few minutes in a match which saw Indian goalkeeper Subrata make an incredible twenty-two saves and deny several golden opportunities to the opposite team.

Baichung replaced the tall and lanky striker Abhishek Yadav in the 78th minute. In the light drizzle and windy conditions that evening in Doha, Baichung lunged and chased the ball. He looked tired and unfit but gave his best shot in his last official match for his country. When Son Heung-Min added Korea's fourth goal in the 81st minute, Baichung looked up towards Doha's dark and overcast sky—it was an expression of disbelief and disappointment.

The 15 minutes he spent on the field before exiting are etched in every Indian football fan's memory.

It was a day of great exits—only 2 minutes before Baichung replaced Yadav, another Asian stalwart, former Manchester

United and Korean skipper Park Ji-Sung walked out after playing his last game for his country.

As a young footballer, Baichung had travelled in unreserved compartments in trains, shared spartan dormitories with teammates, eaten unhygienic food from roadside kiosks, and played tirelessly under the sun and in the rain. The hardships Baichung and other players had gone through during their early years are now well known in India's football circles.

At the end of that tough journey, Baichung believed that he deserved to be part of a tournament as prestigious as the Asian Cup, where India was playing after twenty-seven years.

'I've waited my entire career for a stage like the Asian Cup. To miss it would have been a big disappointment. Even legends and quality players like I.M. Vijayan and Jo Paul Ancheri have never played in the Asian Cup, so I feel a little proud,' Baichung said later.

Houghton agreed wholeheartedly with these sentiments, saying, 'It would have been a great shame if he hadn't had an opportunity to play. He plays for just 20 minutes and it has an effect on the rest of the boys, they all liven up and they all like to play alongside him. He has always been a good influence on his teammates.'

Baichung believed that India's Asian Cup performance had bolstered the national team's image in the international arena and would not be received negatively. It's true to a certain extent. The sizeable Indian community comprises the majority of expats in the oil-rich Gulf state of Qatar. Therefore, the participation of India's national team was seen by many in Doha as something unprecedented—most European expats there had never seen an Indian team take part in a major international event. It did raise the profile of the team on foreign soil, and all the three matches saw a large number of Indian expats in the stadium, egging their team on.

'When we qualified for the Asian Cup in 2008, it was considered a big achievement. Before the Asian Cup, nobody in the Gulf even knew that India had a football team. The event was broadcast everywhere, everybody was talking about Indian football. That's the biggest achievement for us.'

It was unfortunate that he was injured and past his prime when India earned a ticket to the Asian Cup. It's not that the result would have been different for India in the tournament, but a fitter Baichung might have achieved personal glory, like Chhetri who scored two goals in the tournament.

'In Doha, I consulted the Australian team doctor and other local doctors. Every two days, blood clots were drained from my calf and I took painkillers,' recalled Baichung.

In fact, even after the Asian Cup, Baichung nurtured hopes of complete recovery and wanted to continue playing. After consulting the doctor of the Australian team at Doha, he evinced an interest to play in the Asian Cup's 2015 edition as he didn't want to retire as an injured player. But it was not to be.

'I could manage only 15 minutes against South Korea. I wanted to play one last game. But the injury didn't help and it was so frustrating that I decided to put a stop to it.'

At thirty-five, he knew he wouldn't be able to keep up his performance level in competitive football or even at the club level. It was time to say goodbye.

C. Rajshekhar Rao, author of the Indian cricket captain's biography, *Dhoni,* covered Sachin Tendulkar's last Test match in Mumbai in November last year. 'I feel Baichung is to football what Tendulkar is to cricket, at least for our generation. If Tendulkar's performances encouraged parents to get their children to play cricket, I'm sure Baichung must have had his effect too. Though the popularity of cricket is unmatched, I feel football is the only game that can come anywhere near it in the country,' he said.

When the team came back from Doha in mid-January, nobody expected Baichung to continue as a national player. After the Goan Armando Colaco replaced Houghton as the Indian coach, Baichung was dropped for the first time in his career in June 2011. With his list of probables for the 2014 FIFA World Cup qualifier against the United Arab Emirates in July, Colaco signalled a new start for Indian football.

Baichung knew it was all over for him in international football. His dream of playing in the Asian Cup had been fulfilled, but he was no longer considered a force to reckon with.

His last official match for India had been played in Doha in January, and a few months later, in August, he announced his retirement. On 9 January, 2012 he appeared in a testimonial match against Germany's Bayern Munich at Delhi's Nehru Stadium in what was to be his last appearance in the blue shirt.

A day before he played against Bayern, we caught up at a five-star hotel in east Delhi where the Indian team was staying. Baichung was terribly busy. There was a huge media presence and Nike, which had an endorsement deal with Baichung, kept him busy with special photo shoots. One by one, he obliged journalists with interviews, keeping up the same friendly attitude that had won him plaudits.

'We don't get to hear much about Indian football in Germany. We only see Indian cricket. But we all know Baichung since he was part of many World XIs,' said Bayern Munich skipper Philipp Lahm a day before the match.

The Bavarians arrive in India

Bayern Munich, one of the world's most popular clubs from the German city of Munich, travelled to Qatar during their winter break in January 2012. The club chose India as their next destination because the team sponsors, Audi, wanted to tap the automobile market in the country. Besides, their outing against India XI garnered much attention because it was Baichung's farewell match.

The match was held at Delhi's Nehru Stadium, which was packed to capacity on a bitingly cold evening on 9 January, 2012.

Despite not being fully fit, the former India captain gave the 50,000-odd spectators an opportunity to see him don the India colours for the last time.

The contest was a mismatch as a strong Bayern side proved quite a handful for the India XI.

Bayern's Brazilian right-back Rafinha chased Baichung when he had his first touch of the ball in the 2nd minute of the match. Realizing the weaknesses in his team, Baichung fell back in his own half to help the clueless defence. When he took the first shot at the Bayern goal from the top of the box, it felt like a throwback to his heyday as a robust striker.

The German side started with their first XI, except for Franck Ribéry, and toyed with the Indians, attacking at will. The hosts, on the other hand, were content with defending their citadel without even challenging the formidable Bayern defence. That evening, Baichung played with gusto, his commitment motivating his young teammates who played alongside the poster boy of Indian football for the last time.

Finally, an era in Indian football came to an end when C.S. Sabeeth replaced the man from Tinkitam in the 84th minute.

Baichung got a standing ovation. His teammates hugged him and said goodbye to their 'big bro'. It was an emotional end to a glittering career as fans held up banners of 'We Will Miss You' at every corner of the stadium. There was endearing camaraderie from the German players too. Lahm, Bastian

Schweinsteiger and others wished him well and gifted him a No. 15 Bayern Munich jersey that said 'Bhaichung' and had been signed by all the Bayern players.

It didn't really matter that the Germans walked away with a 4–0 verdict, with goals from Mario Gomez (14th minute), Thomas Mueller (29th and 37th minutes) and Schweinsteiger (43rd minute). What impressed everyone was the way the veteran had led the young Indian side in the second session.

Sherap, Baichung's childhood friend and classmate at TNA, who had played for East Bengal in 2001, felt it would be a long time before anyone could fill his shoes. 'The day Baichung retired was a sad one for us. The Indian team now has a new captain but it's very difficult for us to accept that he is not playing any more. Baichung had glamour and star appeal that attracted youngsters to the sport. He had that off-the-field charisma and filling the gap he left will take a long time,' Sherap said.

Many coaches and former players go to the extent of comparing him with another legend and Baichung's idol, I.M. Vijayan. But both these players belonged to two different genres, and choosing between them is like asking who is a better singer—Kishore Kumar or Mohammad Rafi.

Indian coaches Syed Nayeemuddin and Subrata Bhattacharya have said that Vijayan was more talented because the Malayali star played a 'selfless' game. But other coaches such as Houghton and P.K. Banerjee believe that Baichung was the complete package—an intelligent striker, articulate, and possessing great leadership qualities. He saw himself not as an artist but as a winner.

Despite the limited facilities in Indian clubs, Baichung's amazing fitness level had been spectacular and much appreciated by his coaches, including his sharpest critic, Nayeemuddin. Former Bagan coach Karim Bencharifa once said that he had never seen another right-footed player who could strike the ball as cleanly and with such accuracy. His volleys had pace and his headers made life difficult for goalkeepers.

'In a short time, Baichung emerged as a mature striker. He also knew how to carry himself on and off the field, unlike his seniors,' said former India midfielder Tejinder Kumar.

The Nigerian Bernard Oparanozie, a former Mohun Bagan player who later became the club's assistant coach, used to be Baichung's teammate at JCT. Bernard felt that Baichung could have achieved more in his career. 'He didn't get the right support in every team in which he played. Had he got a creative midfielder, Baichung would have scored more goals,' felt Bernard.

He ignited hope

Baichung burst into our national consciousness when Indian football was going through a transition in the early 1990s. His emergence rekindled hope in an Indian team which lacked a star. If his entry into the sport was one of the watershed moments in Indian football, his exit created a stir. After all, there was none who could match his off-field charisma.

'He was a true leader and always led from the front, whether it was in a training session or in a match,' recalled Renedy, who had shared centre stage with Baichung for many years.

Baichung's senior teammate and former India goalkeeper and captain Yousuf Ansari recollected an incident from a 1996 Asian Cup qualifying match against Indonesia in Kuala Lumpur. India's 7–1 defeat was one of the worst in their history, but the young Baichung's steely resolve and determination won hearts. After goalkeeper Arpan Dey got injured, Ansari replaced him in the 32nd minute. But in just 2 minutes, the former Air India goalkeeper was red-carded following a serious infringement on an opponent player. With two of India's goalkeepers out, coach Rustam Akhramov had no other option but to sacrifice one of his midfielders, Ajay Kumar Singh, and substituted him with Baichung at the goal in the 34th minute. Baichung was not in the first eleven as he had high fever, but his teammates were surprised to see the young boy's confidence.

'In fact, he volunteered to be the goalkeeper. He let in three goals, but he was superb. He was an excellent teammate and a great guy who always fought for the team,' said Ansari.

Baichung's positive attitude inspired more than just his team. Apart from hosting the annual Sikkim Governor's Gold Cup since 1979, Sikkim had never been too serious about football. Manipur and Mizoram were more passionate about the game than Sikkim, which only had the late Pem Dorjee playing for India in the early 1980s before Baichung's foray into mainstream football. But Dorjee was a defender unlike

Baichung and played in an era when the electronic media was not so big. Hence, it wouldn't be an exaggeration to say that Baichung had a huge influence on his home state.

A couple of years before Baichung joined East Bengal, Manipur's Kiron Khongsai was already a well-known name from the North-east.

If one traces the history of Indian football, it will be known that Talimeran Ao, who led India's first Olympics football team at the London Games in 1948, was the first player from the North-east to have come down to the plains and joined Mohun Bagan. But it took another thirty-five years to see Dorjee sign up with a Calcutta club, Mohammedan Sporting. Even then, the North-east's representation in the national clubs was marginal or insignificant, dominated as they were by players from Bengal, Punjab, Kerala, Goa, Tamil Nadu, and Karnataka.

After Baichung's arrival, everything changed. Now most of the clubs boast of talented players from Sikkim, Manipur, Mizoram, Nagaland and Meghalaya. Both Sikkim and Indian football got a shot in the arm. Baichung became a role model for young players, a ray of hope for their football dreams.

Baichung's retirement left one such young player, Nim Tshering Lepcha, with a heavy heart. Tshering, who hails from Dzongu in north Sikkim and last year captained United Sikkim FC, saw the former India captain as a symbol of faith, skill, and courage. He was a product of the 'Search for More Baichungs' scheme launched by the Sikkim government in 1999.

The year Baichung retired, three of his India teammates—Mahesh Gawli, Dipak Mondol, and Climax Lawrence—also bid adieu to the game, but the news only found a place in some corner of the sports pages. The press that Baichung's retirement got also reflects his larger-than-life persona in the sport.

Karma Bhutia, who has watched him keenly since his Tinkitam days, followed Baichung's every move on the field during his last game against the German champions. 'For me, his winning the SAFF Cup for the first time in 1997 and his stint in England are the most memorable highlights of his career,' he said.

The road ahead

According to sports psychologist Jack Llewellyn, few professional athletes want to think about coming to the end of their careers while they're still playing. As a consequence, very few of them are prepared for that next chapter.

Retirement is more than the end of a job; it often feels like an inactive life. Not so for Baichung, however. We are not accustomed to seeing a former sportsman play an active role in the development of the sport which he once dominated. How often do you see a former footballer travelling from one part of the country to another to involve himself in the development of the sport? Not often, as it turns out. In that sense, Baichung didn't really retire from the game; he remained immersed in various projects aimed at developing football in his state.

'He has contributed so much to Indian football. I think he is still doing a lot,' said current India captain Sunil Chhetri, who took over the mantle from the man alongside whom he had once played in the national team.

At the end of it all, Baichung remains a man satisfied with a job well done. For him, there has been no dearth of dreams for the past thirty years, ever since he was a kid kicking around a ball in his village in Tinkitam.

9

The Future Beckons

It is hard to imagine the national team without Baichung Bhutia who spent eighteen long years at its heart. Indian football has had its stars, but none whose career took off in such a big way and was so closely linked with technology, reality television, and the celebrity culture. In the era of the Internet and satellite television, Baichung's career was a proven draw; after his retirement, Indian football has been left with a void that has yet to be filled.

'It's difficult to not have him around in the national team. I've never been in a national camp without him for the past seven years,' said the 30-year-old Sunil Chhetri, who equalled Baichung's forty-two goals in international matches for India during a friendly tie against Nepal in November 2013.

While Chhetri is already being hailed as the next torchbearer of Indian football, many feel the Delhi lad is too young to take the place of the icon. Arguably, he is the best player in the current Indian squad, especially having already surpassed Baichung's goal-scoring record for India, but he has miles to go before he can be ranked in the same league as the former India captain.

Baichung's appeal in Indian football has been staggering, be it in his home state or outside. He was not merely a sportsman—he was a brand that blended good looks and charm with athleticism and savvy marketing. The Sikkimese may not have a fancy MBA degree, but his sound understanding of modern sport has helped him position himself uniquely. His engaging personality has helped boost the image of football in cricket-obsessed India, earning him lucrative contracts with leading brands such as Reebok, Adidas, and Nike.

Big screen calling?

In fact, Baichung has behaved every bit like the star he is—he has walked the ramp, danced in a reality show, appeared in various ads, and shared the limelight with world-famous footballers in charity matches internationally. Post-retirement life looks rosy for him now, with much to choose from, including a likely role in a Bollywood movie. Very few know that the 37-year-old appeared in a cameo, playing himself in the Bengali film *Kuasa* (Fog), about a decade ago along with former East Bengal coach Subhash Bhowmick. Years later, having hung up his boots, he is getting offers again to act in films. But nothing has caught his fancy so far.

'Earlier, I was offered guest appearances in movies but didn't consider them as I could not have taken any time out from the game. But now, I would do this only for the sake of an appearance.'

Filmmaker Shoojit Sircar, of *Vicky Donor* and *Madras Café* fame, has met the retired star but Baichung said he is still not clear about the agenda of the meeting. Then he added with typical humility, 'Why would any film producer invest money in me? I'm not a big star.'

Of late, Indian cinema has seen a surge in biographical sports dramas. The success of *Bhaag Milkha Bhaag* has only boosted the appeal of such films. Priyanka Chopra will soon be seen playing Olympian boxer Mary Kom, while there are talks of a film on Sachin Tendulkar as well. The cricket maestro has even reportedly said that if there is a film on him, he would like Aamir Khan to play him.

So, who does Baichung think would do justice to his character if there is a film on him? 'Ranbir Kapoor,' he said without hesitation.

Ask Baichung's wife, Madhuri, and she will tell you just how big a fan of the actor Baichung is. 'Oh, he is just crazy about Ranbir,' she laughed. 'He watches most of Aamir Khan's films as well, but Ranbir probably tops the list among the current crop of actors.'

It would be interesting to see how this star's life would pan out on screen. It sure would give Baichung fans something to cheer about.

Battling the blues

One of the world's best-known basketball players, Kareem Abdul-Jabbar, once said, 'Retirement is the most difficult adjustment because you don't know what to do next.' It is difficult for any star athlete to survive in a world where he could be forgotten by fans and the media. There would be no more autograph-seekers, no more applause, no more front-page photos, and no lucrative product endorsements.

'It hit me hard when I realized that I wouldn't be playing any more. I know people who've been hit by depression when big clubs, good money or the national team bypassed them. It also sounded a bit odd when the media started calling me the former Indian captain as soon as I retired,' Baichung confessed.

Tennis star Björn Borg who retired in 1983, made an attempt to return to the game in the early 1990s. It was unsuccessful and he later filed for bankruptcy. It was only after launching his own fashion brand that he got back upon his feet. Forty-seven-year-old Paul Gascoigne, a former World Cupper who played in the 1990 FIFA World Cup and was once the darling of English fans, is now battling alcoholism. The fame and fortune he enjoyed as a star now seem like a distant memory as he struggles to lead a normal life. Last year, former England and Arsenal star Kenny Sansom was rendered homeless after a life of drinking and gambling.

I.M. Vijayan, according to Baichung, was the greatest star he had the honour of playing with in the national team. In early

2013, the 44-year-old rejoined the Kerala Police team—the same one that had spotted him and taken him under its wing in the late 1980s. After his career ended, Vijayan couldn't come to terms with his post-retirement life, and shuffled between movies, politics, and coaching. His return to Kerala Police seemed to have more to do with him securing a government job rather than indulging his love of the game.

On 19 July, 2006, when former India captain V.P. Sathyan ended his life on a railway track near Chennai at the age of forty-one, we were forced to ask if the sport can offer a better life to retired players.

I had met him once in 2004 at Howrah Municipal Corporation Stadium on the outskirts of Calcutta. His team, Indian Bank, locked horns with Tollygunge Agragami in the NFL. Sathyan, who was equally popular with Mohun Bagan fans when he played alongside I.M. Vijayan in the city in 1991, never looked like someone who would throw himself in front of a train.

On that ill-fated day at Pallavaram railway station in suburban Chennai, nobody paid attention to Sathyan who sat on a bench on platform number 2. Nobody knew what went on in his mind at that moment.

At 11.30 a.m., as a Tambaram-bound train entered the platform, Sathyan jumped in front of it. The sudden death of one of India's leading players left the nation shocked.

Police recovered a suicide note from his pocket, in which he said he was vexed in life as he had lost his wealth and had got habituated to drinking and gambling.

Sathyan's case was a cautionary tale of how depression can plague a former star. Even Diego Maradona had led a disturbed post-retirement life. After being in the limelight for the better part of one's adult life, one has to be mentally strong to lead the life of anonymity that follows retirement. It is essential to channel one's energies and talent constructively.

'Do you drink?' I asked Baichung.

'When I was a player I did drink a few times, but I never behaved stupidly. I always knew there would be a training session the next morning and I shouldn't miss it,' he said. 'Now, even when I've retired, I don't really lead a reckless life.'

In August 2013, a year after his retirement, I caught up with him the day before he left for Manchester as a guest commentator for the English Premier League. I observed how packed his schedule was. 'It's a different life with a different experience. Life has become more hectic than when I was a player. The sad part is that I don't get to be around my kids. I've been really busy ever since I retired,' he said.

Last year, I wanted to meet him one last time before I left for Doha. Baichung was in Thimphu, Bhutan, travelling with United Sikkim FC, which was participating in a tournament. Since he had to stay back in the Bhutanese capital for another two weeks, he asked me to come over to Gangtok on 12 August.

A day later, however, he texted to inform me that the Gorkha Janmukti Morcha had called an indefinite strike in Darjeeling, Siliguri, and the neighbouring areas. As the demand for a separate Gorkhaland intensified and the strike continued, I became a little disappointed.

I had a few more days in Delhi and was wondering where else I could meet Baichung, when he texted me about his proposed visit to the capital. He was leaving for Manchester two days before Independence Day.

I heaved a sigh of relief.

'Let's meet at Ashok hotel in the afternoon,' he said.

Baichung welcomed me with a smile, but he was visibly tired. One look at him and I knew how busy his schedule had been keeping him.

'I would say the journey has just begun and it's not the end of the story,' said Baichung, sitting comfortably on the bed and surfing channels on TV.

We watched the EPL promotions on TV. I was a tad surprised as Indian cricket captain M.S. Dhoni's face appeared on the screen as EPL's brand ambassador. But Baichung displayed no disappointment in the fact that the EPL had picked a cricketer instead of him to promote football. If anything, Baichung was appreciative of the cricket captain's efforts to promote football in Jharkhand.

'The good thing is that Dhoni enjoys and loves sports, including football. He is not just doing endorsements. It comes from his heart. It's great that he is engaged in promoting football,' he said.

I disagreed with Baichung and told him that as a football writer, I could never accept the idea of a cricketer selling football in our country. It meant that we have to see football through the prism of cricket. In that case, basketball legends Michael Jordan and Karim Abdul-Jabbar—not Maradona—should promote football in North America.

As the discussion stretched, Baichung became animated, ignoring the discomfort in his sprained neck as he explained how the two sports differ in the country.

'In India, cricket sells. And I'm not a big star like the cricketers. It's all about marketing: whoever is more saleable will be in demand.

'Unless you succeed at the international level, you don't have that kind of coverage, and you don't get any sponsors. Cricket has been doing that. So we've got to look into what we can learn from cricket and incorporate it into our game,' he said. He was happy to have been selected as one of the Hindi commentators for the EPL. Although he had earlier been an English commentator on Ten Sports during the 2002 World Cup, he did not have any reservations about doing the same in Hindi.

'It's our national language. I don't mind at all. After all, the channel wants to promote the game even in far-off areas where people understand only Hindi,' he said.

In the context of transition, Baichung seems to have adjusted well. His brand value has remained intact, still very much in demand with social organizations, schools, the corporate sector and even, as the elections showed, with West

Bengal's firebrand chief minister. He has followed his passion single-mindedly, which keeps him in the thick of things. His post-retirement life has not been defined solely by football. He has engaged himself in other activities, organizing benefit matches for quake-hit Sikkim or generously contributing to social causes. While Baichung's predecessors led their post-retirement life either in obscurity or in regular ten-to-five jobs—mostly in banks or PSUs—Baichung was sharp enough to understand the realities of life after football. He had a clear idea of where to invest his time and money.

United Sikkim and football school

Like a seasoned entrepreneur, he invested a part of his earnings in his club and diverted some of it to set up BB Studio, a fitness centre in the heart of Gangtok in February 2013. Right from the start of his career, Baichung had clarity on his future. He never wanted to depend on the pension from the Arjuna or Padma Shri awards. Always enterprising, he understood the importance of keeping himself in the 'thick of the action' once he retired from the game.

'You must have some sense of responsibility because you know you have a family and you have to look after them,' he quipped.

In October 2010, during the Commonwealth Games in Delhi, I got a surprise call from Baichung. He evinced keen interest to launch his first football school—the Baichung Bhutia Football School—in the capital.

'Can you help me launch the school in Delhi?' he asked.

I suggested that he postpone the date till after the Commonwealth Games as the international event would steal the thunder of the launch of his school. He agreed and, on 30 October, 2010, he kicked off BBFS in Delhi, and opened another in Mumbai a few months later.

Though the schools keep him busy, it is United Sikkim that has been taking up much of his time. He wants to build a team good enough to qualify for the I-League. With that aim in mind, he has an uphill battle to fight, which includes getting gas and cable connections for his players. Baichung is completely hands-on with the team and when his club didn't have a full-time coach, he coached the players himself, stepping down when the Aussie Nathan Hall joined them on 8 December, 2012.

'If he decides to do something, he will do it. He'll never shy away from his commitments. He'll complete any task that he takes up,' said his sister Kunzang proudly.

In March 2011, two months after he returned from the Asian Cup in Doha, when he introduced himself as the CEO of Sikkim United at a launch programme in Calcutta, there was no doubt that he had been accepted and welcomed in his new role. Baichung even had Dhoni's support. Singer–composer Shankar Mahadevan and Dubai-based FidelisWorld, a newbie sports and entertainment company, became his partners to help him attain his goal.

By 2011, Baichung had taken on the mantle of an entrepreneur. He had never wanted to involve himself in player management and work as a football agent and, therefore, slipped into his new role with confidence and ease.

Nurturing a bunch of talented players needs hard work and sacrifice and in this respect Baichung can be compared to his mentor, Karma Bhutia, and Achyut Banerjee, who devoted their time to spotting and encouraging young footballers from far-flung areas.

Baichung was different from the rest in another respect too. Awards were to be cherished when they came his way, but Baichung never actively tried to make them happen. I know of former sports stars who single-mindedly focussed their energies on the Arjuna Awards once they retired and were seen spending a lot of time with their state ministers and AIFF officials. Two famous Indian footballers of the 1980s and one of Baichung's teammates chased their respective ministers for the Arjuna Awards, but none took up the challenge of involving themselves in the promotion and betterment of the game. Though it would be easy to point fingers, the fact is that there exists a great sense of insecurity among non-cricketing heroes in our country. It worked to Baichung's advantage that he did not concern himself with laurels. As his teachers pointed out, he was always one to put his mind to the task at hand and perform without thinking about the end result. That quality helped him keep insecurities at bay and immerse himself constructively in the game. There are moments of doubt, though. 'At times, I think I could have achieved more,' he said. A thought echoed by Syed Nayeemuddin, who once said, 'He was a terrific player, but I think he should have attained a greater status than what he has got.'

Baichung's contribution to his state

United Sikkim's primary aim was to promote the game in Baichung's own state as the star had always played outside Sikkim during his career. He wanted to make the club a market-oriented and professional team whose visibility stretched beyond the boundaries of Sikkim. He enlisted Bollywood star Ranbir Kapoor as the club's brand ambassador, and, making the most of his rapport with national players, he got Renedy and N.S. Manju to play alongside him for his club in the I-League Second Division. With Baichung at the helm, Nike also thought it would make good business sense to sponsor the team.

In its first year, United Sikkim signed thirty players, including four foreigners, eleven from Sikkim, one from Darjeeling, and a few others from across the country. The first batch trained in Calcutta under coach Stanley Rozario, a former assistant to Bob Houghton in the Indian team.

Baichung became United Sikkim's owner, director, coach, player, and marketing manager all rolled into one, and the team debuted in Indian football with a match against Shillong's Langsning Sports Club at Guwahati's Nehru Stadium on 1 April, 2011. It set the ball rolling for his club.

Appreciating Baichung's love and passion for football, Dhoni said: 'I thank Bhaichung for what he has done for Sikkim and the nation.'

Baichung shifted with his family from Calcutta to Gangtok so that he could spend more time with his club and remain actively involved in the development of the game. The club qualified for the I-League's 2011–12 season, but the debut was painful as the team nosedived. Sherap, however, observed that despite United Sikkim's failure in its maiden year, interest in the game was revived in the state.

'Top clubs came to Gangtok's Paljor Stadium to play United Sikkim in the I-League. It brought back the crowds and got youngsters interested in the sport once again. On a personal note, Baichung has taken a huge risk by investing his hard-earned money in the club. This is his way of contributing to Indian football after retirement,' explained Sherap.

Unfortunately, with no big sponsors keen to support it, United Sikkim is now cash-strapped. This, however, has not shaken Baichung's confidence and he doesn't intend to shut shop like JCT and Mahindra United did in 2009–10.

'It's quite difficult to convince someone to invest in football,' Baichung added. With no money available to strengthen the team, Baichung intends to follow a long-term strategy for the club: invest in youth. By identifying and grooming talented schoolboys, United Sikkim aims to create a pool of skilled players, not just for the team, but also for the country.

Though Baichung never evinced any interest to join the AIFF, preferring to involve himself with his club instead, he was appointed chairman of the federation's Technical Committee in April 2013. It marked his foray into sports administration. AIFF's decision came as no surprise, as Baichung's presence would give the federation some much-needed glamour and attention.

His new role as AIFF Technical Committee chairman means that Baichung still has to travel a lot. He interacts with AIFF academy coaches and officials, and lends his support to improve the sport at the grass-roots level.

I-League vs ISL

While concentrating on the growth of the game in his state, Baichung is also keen to improve the structure of the I-League, the country's premier event, which he feels has become boring and lacks a marketing edge. Such flaws, according to him, are some of the reasons why the Indian youth is more keen on watching European leagues on TV rather than going to stadiums. Hence, it came as no surprise when he endorsed AIFF's idea to launch the IMG-Reliance-sponsored Indian Super League (ISL). When most club owners and former players criticized the national body, he came out in support of the new venture.

'I-League has not been able to create the necessary impact. Indian football has not really progressed and the IMG-Reliance tournament is an excellent concept which can attract stakeholders,' he said.

While Baichung remains one of the staunch supporters of ISL, which offers around Rs 35 crore, there are doubts about the game's growth in the country. Most experts feel—and this is a view I second—that the participation of retired world stars in the inaugural event won't make much of a difference to the sport. Just as cricket writers in the late 1970s dubbed the one-day series by Kerry Packer as 'pajama cricket', the ISL is nothing more than a money-churning gimmick hijacked by AIFF from a Calcutta-based celebrity management group.

The ISL, which is set to kick off in September 2014 and run till November, has been conceptualized on the lines of cricket's Indian Premier League (IPL). It will have eight franchises, with each team featuring one major marquee player. Fifty-nine Indian players have already been signed. There is a touch of glamour from Bollywood and the world of cricket too, with Salman Khan, John Abraham, Ranbir Kapoor, Sachin Tendulkar, and Sourav Ganguly all joining the bandwagon as owners of the franchise teams. But the tournament has been criticized by many observers for the threat it poses to the existing I-League.

Worldwide, football has seen mixed fortunes. In Indonesia, after corruption in the country's football federation surfaced, a breakaway league with Microsoft and Coca-Cola backfired. China couldn't quite take its football to the desired level despite big money. But there are also the examples of Japan, South Korea and Australia, where huge money, backed by a proper plan, has turned around the country's football fortunes.

The ISL is about quality, but given that Indian football struggles from a lack of fans and finance, the cash-rich event can do a world of good only if it injects both energy and money into development at the grass-roots level.

Madhuri is happy that her husband has hung up his boots because she was worried about his niggling knee injury. All Baichung wants to do, however, is be on the football field whenever he can. Once he travelled from Delhi to Jharkhand and returned on the same day—all to be on the turf for a total of 15 minutes in Ranchi.

It does look like he has a lot on his plate; he travels often, shuttling from city to city—Gangtok, Darjeeling, Siliguri, Delhi, Mumbai, and Calcutta.

'How many footballers are interested in doing something for the game once they retire?' asked Sherap. 'He's different from the rest. He's still a star who has been contributing in whatever way he can.'

Baichung attends as many football promotions and seminars as he can, and shares his experiences. However, for all the new areas he has been exploring, Baichung still misses being a player.

Today, having already worn the hat of a successful entrepreneur, he also has plans for a coffee shop and lounge in Gangtok, as well as for marketing football merchandise. Often, Baichung is seen at FPAI annual functions to honour players or at NGO programmes to encourage underprivileged children to take up football.

Reminiscing about his days as a struggling sportsperson, the erstwhile poster boy of Indian football said that he was lucky to have got into professional football while still in school.

'Schools and colleges do not have the kind of infrastructure needed to promote talent when that is the need of the hour in the current context,' he said.

Guided by him, Baichung Bhutia Football School has been taking part in promotional events to encourage football in schools and colleges. Last year, it tied up with Nirmal Lifestyle to introduce the concept of university football league, modelled on current international university sports leagues, like in the US and England.

Baichung's positive approach to retirement has broken many myths and stereotypes. He does not crib about the lack of support from the game's administrative bodies to former players. Instead of praying for handouts or investing unwisely, Baichung has managed to turn his positives into assets, generating more goodwill and currency out of them than is expected of a retired sportsperson in India. Perhaps it was the horror stories of penury-stricken Olympians or hopelessly lost players that spurred him on, but there is no denying Baichung's determination to take control of his own destiny.

At the time of writing this, Baichung, his plate already full, was being approached for *Bigg Boss* and *Survivor India*. Where most others might have jumped at the chance to be back in the limelight, Baichung is particular about being seen for the right things. And now, as it has been for most of his adult life, his focus is a rectangular pitch with goalposts at both ends.

There have been stars before him, of course. Pem Dorjee, Kul Bahadur Chettri, and Karma Lodey Bhutia were perhaps some of the best Sikkimese players who have represented the country, but nobody could make a bigger impact than him. His work ethics and popularity have inspired and encouraged a whole generation in his state.

Karma Yougyal, a retired joint director of the department of sports and youth affairs, Sikkim government, who conceived of and started the 'Search for More Baichungs' campaign, said, 'I appreciate Baichung and his determination to promote the game in his state. I hope his club will give more opportunities to Sikkimese players.'

Baichung has been a role model to many young footballers from his state who now represent various clubs and different age-group teams of the national squad. Sanju Pradhan and Nirmal Chettri are key members in the Indian senior team today, while Bikash Jairu, Robin Gurung, Santu Subba, Sanjay Chettri, Nim Tshering Lepcha, Sagar Rai, and Nim Dorjee Tamang are dynamic players donning the colours of various premier clubs in the country.

He may have retired from the pitch, but he has certainly not retired from football or from his brand. With his strength of character and conviction, his clarity of purpose and passion, Baichung is charting a course that will have an impact not only at a personal level but also at the national and perhaps international levels.

His footprints will be felt on the turf long after he has stepped off it for good.

Fast Facts

Date of birth: 15 December, 1976
Place: Tinkitam, Sikkim

Playing career
International caps: 107
Goals: 42

Debut
Versus Thailand in 1995 Nehru Cup in Kolkata as a substitute for Shabbir Pasha.

First international goal
Versus Uzbekistan in 1995 Nehru Cup in Kolkata. India won 1–0.

International tournaments

1. World Cup qualifiers: 1996, 2001, 2004, 2007
2. Asia Cup finals: 2011
3. Asia Cup qualifiers: 1996, 2006
4. Pre-Olympic qualifiers: 1995
5. Asian Games: 1998, 2002, 2006
6. Nehru Cup: 1995, 1997, 2007, 2009
7. Afro-Asian Games: 2003
8. LG Cup: 2002, 2004

Trophies won

1. AFC Challenge Cup: 2008
2. Nehru Cup: 2007, 2009
3. SAFF Cup: 1997, 1999, 2005
4. SAF Games: 1995
5. LG Cup: 2002

Most Valuable Player

AFC Challenge Cup in 2008. Scored three goals in the tournament, including one in the final.

Player of the Tournament

Nehru Cup 2009 (scored two goals and won two Man of the Match awards); SAFF Cup 1999 and 2005.

Record

Has scored 12 goals, highest by an Indian in SAFF Cup.

Club career

1. Tashi Namgyal Academy, Gangtok, 1987, 1988, 1989
2. SAI Centre, Gangtok/Sikkim Blues: 1990, 1991, 1992
3. East Bengal: 1993, 1994, 1995, 1997, 1998, 2003, 2004, 2005, 2009
4. JCT: 1996
5. Bury FC (England): 1999, 2000, 2001
6. Mohun Bagan: 2002, 2006, 2007, 2008 (captain)
7. Perak FC (Malaysia): 2003
8. United Sikkim: 2010, 2011

Goals scored: 228

1. East Bengal: 148
2. Mohun Bagan: 46
3. JCT: 25
4. Perak FC: 4
5. Bury FC: 3
6. Sikkim Blues: 1
7. United Sikkim: 1

State appearances

Played for Bengal in Santosh Trophy in 1994, 1996, 1997 and led the team in 1998. Bengal won the trophy on all four occasions and Baichung scored 12 goals.

Club trophies won

1. LG ASEAN Club Cup: 2003 Jakarta
2. Wai Wai Cup: 1993 Kathmandu

3. National Football League (I-League): 1996–97, 2003–04
4. Federation Cup: 2006, 2008, 2009
5. Kolkata League: 1993, 1995, 1998, 2003, 2004, 2007, 2008
6. IFA Shield: 1994, 1995, 1996, 2004
7. Durand Cup: 1993, 1995, 1996, 2004
8. Rovers Cup: 1994

Honours

1. Padma Shri: 2008
2. Arjuna Award: 1998
3. AIFF Player of the Year: 1995, 2008

Golden Boot

1. National Football League, 1996–97
2. Federation Cup, 1995, 1996, 2006
3. LG ASEAN Cup, 2003
4. Kolkata League 1994

Other achievements

Best player: National Football League (2005–06)
Best striker: National Football League (2005–06, 12 goals)

Acknowledgements

I have many people to thank for their assistance and cooperation in the writing of this book, first among those include my friend C. Rajshekhar Rao. The proposed biography gained pace when Rajshekhar insisted that I must finish it because Baichung deserves it.

Kanishka Gupta's editorial suggestions also played a key role in giving shape to the book.

Sincere thanks are also due to Kunzang, Baichung's sister, mentor Karma Bhutia, teacher Leonard Lefevre and friend Sherap Lepcha. In fact, all of them brought out Baichung's early years as a child.

Steve Darby, his former coach at Mohun Bagan; his former teammates Bernard Oparanozie, Tejinder Kumar, Stephen Abarowei, Godfred Pereira; coaches Amal Dutta, Shyamal Ghosh and Bhaskar Ganguly, who introduced him to East Bengal, all deserve big thanks for helping with their inputs.

Thanks to Oliver Kay, chief football correspondent, the *Times*, UK, for his insights on Baichung's stint with Bury FC.

I must mention my artist friend Riyas Komu for providing the cover picture. Also, a big thanks to Jatin V. Paranjape and Sameer Tamhane.

I also appreciate the support and encouragement I got from my family members and friends.

A Note on the Author

Mohammad Amin-ul Islam was born on 15 December, 1971 in Calcutta, where he began his career as a freelancer with *The Statesman* in 1993 and later joined the now defunct *Amrita Bazar Patrika* in 1995. A year later he relocated to New Delhi to work with *The Asian Age, The Pioneer, The Indian Express, Zee Sports* and *The Times of India,* where he worked for six years before moving to Doha, Qatar, in 2012.

Kunzang

Baichung, aged six, with his parents, Sonam Topden Bhutia and Dorji Doma Bhutia.

Baichung, standing second from right, in his first-ever football match for St Xavier's School.

Kunzang

Leonard Lefevre

From the Tashi Namgyal Academy album.

Kunzang

Baichung, sitting second from right, with St Xavier's classmates.

From the Tashi Namgyal Academy album.

Leonard Lefevre

Kunzang

Baichung, extreme left, during a school tour with Tashi Namgyal Academy teammates.

Leonard Lefevre

Whenever he came to Sikkim from Calcutta, Baichung made sure he met his school teachers at Tashi Namgyal Academy.

Leonard Lefevre

Baichung with his former teacher Leonard Lefevre, third from left, during an inter-school tournament.

Leonard Lefevre

Baichung as chief guest with his former teacher Leonard Lefevre, sitting third from right, during a school tournament in Gangtok.

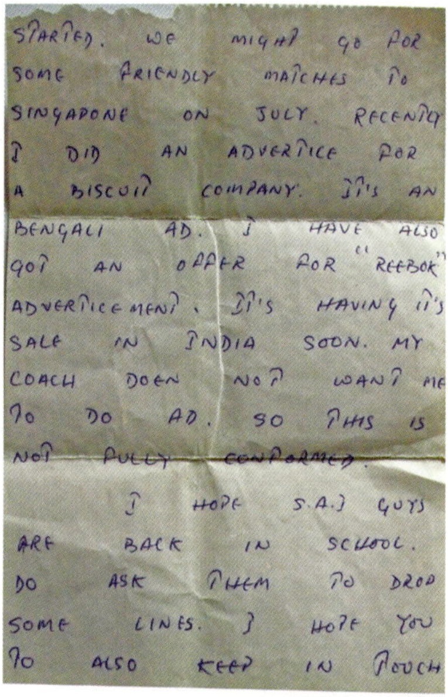

STARTED. WE MIGHT GO FOR SOME FRIENDLY MATCHES TO SINGAPORE ON JULY. RECENTLY I DID AN ADVERTICE FOR A BISCUIT COMPANY. IT'S AN BENGALI AD. I HAVE ALSO GOT AN OFFER FOR "REEBOK" ADVERTICEMENT. IT'S HAVING IT'S SALE IN INDIA SOON. MY COACH DOEN NOT WANT ME TO DO AD. SO THIS IS NOT FULLY CONFORMED.

I HOPE S.A.I GUYS ARE BACK IN SCHOOL. DO ASK THEM TO DROP SOME LINES. I HOPE YOU TO ALSO KEEP IN TOUCH

Leonard Lefevre

After Baichung left Sikkim in 1993, he made it a point to write letters to his favourite teacher 'Lenny Sir' about his daily activities in Calcutta.

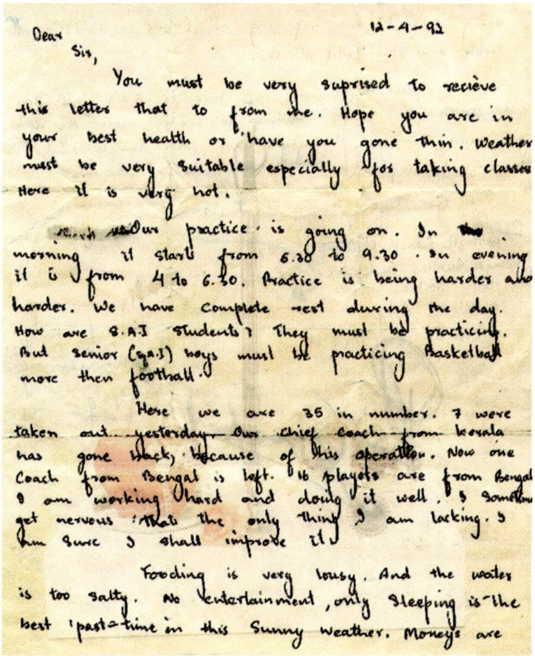

12-4-92

Dear Sir,

You must be very suprised to recieve this letter that to from me. Hope you are in your best health or have you gone thin. Weather must be very suitable especially for taking classes Here it is very hot.

Our practice is going on. In morning it starts from 6.30 to 9.30. In evening it is from 4 to 6.30. Practice is being harder and harder. We have complete rest during the day. How are S.A.I students? They must be practicing. But senior (S.A.I) boys must be practicing Basketball more then football.

Here we are 35 in number. 7 were taken out yesterday. Our chief coach from Kerala has gone back, because of his operation. Now one Coach from Bengal is left. 16 players are from Bengal. I am working hard and doing it well. I sometimes get nervous, that's the only thing I am lacking. I am sure I shall improve it.

Fooding is very lousy. And the water is too salty. No entertainment, only sleeping is the best 'past-time' in this sunny weather. Moneys are being wasted be repairing new (made in Hari) football boots and on Cold drinks.

Please Convey my love to S.A.I footballers and Deven. I have nothing to write more. By now you must be very hungry. Have your lunch and have only 3 plates.

Goodbye Namasta Salaam Sasriakal

My add.
Football Coaching Camp
Netaji Subhas Eastern Centre
Boys Hostel
Saltlake City
Calcutta 700091

Yours fatefully
Bhaichung
Vega

IF YOU FEEL LIKE WRITTIN TO ME THEN ADD, IS WITH MR. MANASH OR YOU CAN TAKE FROM HOSTEL GUYS.

20th MAY 93

DEAR SIR,

HOPE YOU WOULD BE VERY SUPRISE TO RECIEVE MY LETTER. I WAS JUST THINKING OF S.A.I GUYS, SINCE THEY MUST HAVE LEFT FOR COACHING CAMP, YOU MUST BE FELING BORED WITHOUT THEM. ANYWAY, I HOPE YOU TO BE IN YOUR BEST HEALTH.

HERE I AM VERY BUSY WITH MY PRACTICE MORE THEN THINKING OF MY RESULTS. YOU MUST BE KNOWING THAT I AM IN INDIA - U-19 COACHING CAMP. I HAVE NOT YET STARTED MY PRACTICE WITH CLUB, SINCE I AM NOT FREE FROM THE CAMP. MOREOVER I AM DOING WELL. CAMP IS ENDING ON 24th MAY. AGAIN ON 4th JUNE WE ARE GOING TO PLAY AT KATHMANDU. (EAST BENGAL).

ABOUT MY HOUSE IT IS NOT YET BEEN FIXED. HOPE TO GET IT NEAR THE GROUND (EAST BENGAL). AND SCHOOLING, I SHALL DO IT IN NEARBY ONCE. SINCE OUR PRACTICE FINISHES ON 10.a.m SO I HAVE TO REACH THE SCHOOL ALSO ON TIME.

SO I HOPE, EVERYONE IS FINE OUT THERE. DO GIVE MY LOVE TO OTHER TEACHER'S ALSO. SINCE IT'S GETTING LATE FOR ME TO CHANGE AND GO FOR PRACTICE, I SHALL END IT HERE ITSELF. I HOPE YOU DON'T MIND WRITTING YOU SHORT AND ALSO COPING YOUR HANDWRITTING. GOODBYE.

WITH REGARDS
B. HAICHUNG.

EAR 'SIR',   24TH JUNE 95.

I'M VERY THANKFUL YOU FOR REMEMBERING ME. THOUGHT BY NOW ALL NACIANS HAS FORGOTTEN ME. . HARDLY RECIEVE ANY LETTER OM THE GUYS, I TOO I VERY LAZY, COZ I DON'T RITE FIRST, I ONLY REPLY. HOPE EVERYONE IS KEEPING NE. PRINCI MUST BE VERY LAXED ALSO.

I HEARD MR. MANASH AS BEEN TRANSFERED. IF NOT HEN, DO GIVE MY WARM EGARDS TO HIM AND HIS AMILY. HERE OUR PRACTICES R PRE-OLYMPIC GAME HAS STARTED. WE MIGHT GO FOR SOME FRIENDLY MATCHES TO SINGAPORE ON JULY. RECENTLY I DID AN ADVERTICE FOR A BISCUIT COMPANY. IT'S AN BENGALI AD. I HAVE ALSO GOT AN OFFER FOR "REEBOK" ADVERTICEMENT. IT'S HAVING IT'S SALE IN INDIA SOON. MY COACH DOES NOT WANT ME TO DO AD. SO THIS IS NOT FULLY CONFORMED.

I HOPE S.A.I GUYS ARE BACK IN SCHOOL. DO ASK THEM TO DROP SOME LINES. I HOPE YOU TO ALSO KEEP IN TOUCH.

LASTLY DO GIVE MY WARM REGARDS TO ALL THE TEACHERS AND STUDENT. (ESPECIALLY IN BIO-CLASSES). I MIGHT TURN UP ON AUGUST. HOPE YOU TO BE IN GANGTOK ONLY. TILL THEN BYE.

CIAO.

YOUR'S EX STUDENT,

BHAICHUNG.

Baichung Bhutia Facebook page

With cricket maestro Sachin Tendulkar at a Calcutta hotel in 1995.

Wearing jersey No.15, which is his date of birth, Baichung walked into the hearts of millions of Indian fans when he debuted in the 1995 Nehru Cup in Calcutta. Here he is seen with former India coach Rustam Akhramov.

Raman Vijayan

The Indian team's victory lap after winning the SAFF Cup in Kathmandu, Nepal, 1997.

Raman Vijayan

Baichung, standing seventh from right, with the 1998 Bangkok Asian Games squad.

Baichung, standing second from left, with the Indian team which won the LG Cup in Vietnam in 2002.

Luis Arruda/Football & Friends

The Indian team at Agueda, Portugal in 2007.

Rajeev Tyagi

Baichung flanked by Syed Rahim Nabi, K. Ajayan, Sanjeev Maria and Sandip Nandy at the Nehru Cup camp at Delhi's Ambedkar Stadium, 2007.

Anindya Chattopadhyay

Baichung celebrates a goal against Turkmenistan in the 2009 Nehru Cup.

Anindya Chattopadhyay

Baichung celebrates India's Nehru Cup victory at Delhi's Ambedkar Stadium, 2009.

Anindya Chattopadhyay

Baichung celebrates India's Nehru Cup victory at Delhi's Ambedkar Stadium, 2009.

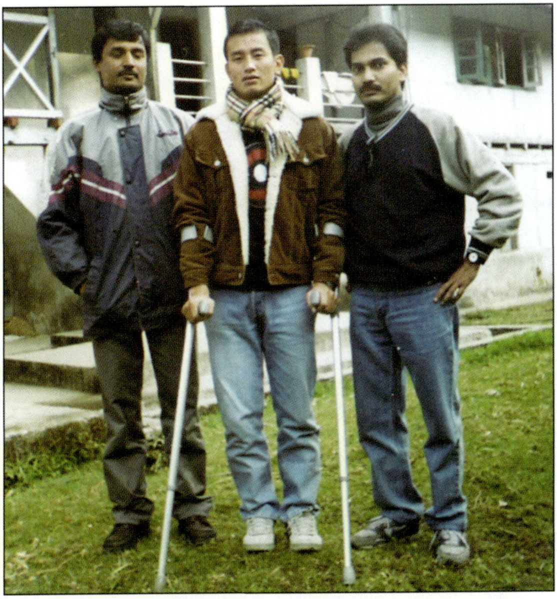

Mohammad Amin-ul Islam

Baichung with the author, right, and a fan, at Tinkitam.

Mohammad Amin-ul Islam

The Sikkim Government honoured their famous son with a stadium at Namchi.

Mohammad Amin-ul Islam

Baichung seen here with his father, Sonam Topden Bhutia, and mother, Dorji Doma Bhutia, in this photograph. Baichung always said that whenever he found time from his hectic football schedule in Calcutta, he would rush to his village and recharge himself in Tinkitam's quieter surroundings.

Kunzang

Newly-weds Baichung and Madhuri take part in a traditional Sikkimese dance.

At the reception with his footballer friends who once played with him in the Boys Club.

Blessings from the Rimpoche in the family prayer room at Tinkitam.

Mohammad Amin-ul Islam

Former coach Bob Houghton, second from right, instructs players before India's match against South Korea in the 2011 Asian Cup in Doha.

AKB

South Korea's Lee Young-pyo challenges Baichung in his last official international match in the 2011 Asian Cup in Doha.

Arjun Rai

Bob Houghton compared him with cricketing legend Sachin Tendulkar. Here he is seen with Tendulkar, left, and friend Arjun Rai in Dubai.

Anindya Chattopadhyay

Baichung trains with India teammates in Delhi.

Baichung always maintained that he has the deepest regard for Bob Houghton.

Anindya Chattopadhyay

USFC

Baichung with musician Shankar Mahadevan, left, at the launch of United Sikkim Football Club in Calcutta, 2011.

Rajeev Tyagi

Baichung in a lighter mood.

Baiching waves to his fans after his farewell match against Bayern Munich.

Rajeev Tyagi

Rajeev Tyagi

Germany and Bayern Munich skipper Philip Lahm presents his team jersey to Baichung in New Delhi in 2012.

Rajeev Tyagi

Baichung is challenged by Franck Ribery, right, in the match.

Sikkim Express

Baichung interacts with the public during the 15th Lok Sabha campaign at Kalimpong and Darjeeling.

Sikkim Express

Sikkim Express

Baichung wanted to work for the people of the hills. But his dream remains unfulfilled as he lost the Lok Sabha election from Darjeeling. Here he is seen with tea garden workers at the Dooars.

FPAI

Baichung shares the dais with, from left, Renedy Singh, P.K. Banerjee, and West Bengal Governor M.K. Narayanan at the Football Players Association of India annual awards in Calcutta, April, 2014.

Madhuri Tipnis Bhutia

Madhuri Tipnis Bhutia

Whenever Baichung is back in Sikkim, he spends quality time with his kids, Ugen, Keisha, and Samara.